If you find this book, either
enjoy it yourself or return to...

_____

_____

_____

_____

Published by LifeWay Press®
© 2013 LifeWay Press
Reprinted 2013

No part of this work may be reproduced or transmitted in any form or by any means, electronic or mechanical, including photocopying and recording, or by any information storage or retrieval system, except as may be expressly permitted in writing by the publisher. Requests for permission should be addressed in writing to LifeWay Press®, One LifeWay Plaza, Nashville, TN 37234-0135.

ISBN: 978-1-4158-7970-2
Item: 005560882

Dewey Decimal Classification Number: 269.2
Subject Heading: EVANGELISTIC WORK \ WITNESSING \ GOSPEL

Printed in the United States of America.

Young Adult Ministry Publishing
LifeWay Church Resources
One LifeWay Plaza
Nashville, Tennessee 37234-0135

We believe that the Bible has God for its author; salvation for its end; and truth, without any mixture of error, for its matter and that all Scripture is totally true and trustworthy. To review LifeWay's doctrinal guideline, please visit *www.lifeway.com/doctrinalguideline.*

Cover design by Eric Pavol

TABLE OF CONTENTS

ABOUT THE AUTHORS

J.D. GREEAR is the lead pastor of The Summit Church, in Raleigh-Durham, North Carolina, and author of *Gospel: Recovering the Power that Made Christianity Revolutionary* (2011) and *Stop Asking Jesus into Your Heart: How to Know for Sure You Are Saved* (2013). God has blessed The Summit Church with tremendous growth. Under J.D.'s leadership, the Summit has grown from a plateaued church of 300 to one of nearly 8,000, making it one of Outreach magazine's "top 25 fastest-growing churches in America" for several years running. He and his wife Veronica live in Raleigh and are raising four kids: Kharis, Alethia, Ryah, and Adon.

J.D. completed his Ph.D. in Theology at Southeastern Baptist Theological Seminary where he is also a faculty member, writing on the correlations between early church presentations of the gospel and Islamic theology. Having lived and served among Muslims, he has a burden to see them, as well as every nation on earth, come to know and love the salvation of God in Christ.

ROB TURNER is teaching pastor and team lead over Gathering Ministries at Apex Community Church in Kettering, Ohio. He holds a MDiv in Missions, Evangelism, and Church Growth and a PhD in Leadership from Southern Baptist Theological Seminary. Rob is also an associate professor at Cedarville University.

The mission of his life is to delight in Jesus so much that he would be compelled to love, equip, and send people for the fame of Christ's name. In addition to preaching, Rob is part of one of Apex Community's missional communities that are networked throughout the Miami Valley of Ohio. These communities meet each week to make much of Jesus through the Scriptures, intentional relationships, and reaching unbelievers in the geographical context. Rob and his wife Angela live in Dayton, Ohio, with their four children. You can find him on Facebook and on Twitter @ApexPastorBoy.

DERWIN GRAY is the founding and lead pastor of Transformation Church, a multi-ethnic, multi-generational, mission-shaped community in Indian Land, South Carolina, just south of Charlotte, North Carolina, Transformation Church was named the 2nd fastest growing church by percentage and the 14th fastest growing church by number of participants in America in 2010, according to Outreach magazine. Derwin and his wife Vicki have been married for 20 years and have two children, Presley and Jeremiah.

After graduating from Brigham Young University, Derwin played in the NFL for five years with the Indianapolis Colts (1993-1997) and one year with the Carolina Panthers (1998). During that time, he and Vicki experienced God's faithfulness and direction as He moved their hearts to know Him and make Him known. Derwin went on to graduate from Southern Evangelical Seminary with a Master of Divinity (M.Div.) in apologetics. Lovingly known as the "Evangelism Linebacker," learn more about Derwin on his blog, Just Marinating.

BEN REED is the small groups pastor at Long Hollow, a multi-site church in the Nashville, Tennessee, area. Ben and his wife have been married for 9 years and have a 4-year-old son. Ben completed his MDiv in Biblical Counseling from Southern Baptist Theological Seminary. Before he graduated, though, he stepped into small groups ministry and has never looked back. He's helped launch hundreds of small groups, releasing people to jump into healthy, authentic community.

Ben serves as an editorial advisor to Christianity Today's *smallgroups.com*, an editorial advisor to Right Now Media, and has written for *Outreach* magazine and *Collegiate* magazine. He's a regular contributor at *pastors.com* and *churchleaders.com*, and has been featured in *The Christian Post*. In addition to pastoring, preaching, and writing, Ben has a great passion for coffee. Good coffee, that is. And CrossFit. But not at the same time. You can journey along with Ben at *BenReed.net*

Engage.

Preparing to make disciples

The Roman Road. F.A.I.T.H. Four Spiritual Laws.

These are all names of good, useful tools for evangelism—some that we'll even walk through in this study. Yet the goal of each tool is to introduce someone to a relationship with Jesus Christ in a simple, straight-forward way. And these tools have worked really well. But in today's times, evangelism is directly connected to relationships. We crave depth in all aspects of life, whether in interactions with others, our daily experiences, or in our faith.

Unbelievers are looking for real answers not easy ones. They're wanting to see that men and women of faith struggle with questions, too. They're looking for a belief system that actually has something to say. That also means, however, that people are looking for a belief system that demands something. They're looking for something challenging, something that will engage their whole person— body, mind, and spirit. They don't want Christians to try and "back-door" the gospel to them; say what it is, and be up-front about it. It's a complete life commitment, and something worth giving your whole life toward.

That means that evangelism and discipleship go hand in hand. It's not minimizing the need for the moment of truth—when a person steps from being an unbeliever to believer— because there's still the profound need for that. But it does mean that perhaps the best evangelism plan is to show people the gospel lived out, engaging in worship and study.

In this resource, you're not going to simply get tools that will help you share your faith. We don't believe that tools are the only thing you need. Sharing our faith requires reminders of the beauty and depth of the gospel, how to defend that gospel, and why we need to share it. And since sharing with others is personal and unique, we've asked four different authors with varying backgrounds and personalities to help guide us through that framework of healthy relationships.

How to Use This Book

What better way to learn about sharing the gospel than in community with others? That's why we've designed *Engage* as a small group Bible study. Geared for a no-prep small group experience, this study is intended to be facilitator led with a strong discussion focus. In each session you'll find:

- Questions to help you and/or your group process the Scriptures and content of each session

- Facilitator tips (*) to help effectively lead the gathering

- A "This Week…" section at the close of each session to allow you to reflect on what was learned and put the session into practice in your personal life.

What exactly is "the gospel"?

by J.D. Greear

"I want you to see the gospel not only as the means by which you get into heaven, but as the driving force behind every single moment of your life. . . . I want you to see how the gospel, and it alone, can make you genuinely passionate for God, free you from captivity to sin, and move you outward to joyful sacrifice on behalf of others."
—J.D. Greear, *Gospel: Recovering the Power that Made Christianity Revolutionary*[1]

It sounds simple. You've probably heard "the gospel" many times, but what does it really mean? Before we dive in, take a moment to ponder that this single question may be the most important one you'll ever consider.

Paul said the gospel was the power of God for salvation, the only means by which we can have peace with God.

> "For I am not ashamed of the gospel, because it is God's power for salvation to everyone who believes, first to the Jew, and also to the Greek" (Romans 1:16).

Paul thought it was worth giving his life for, something he would eventually do. He believed its contents were so essential that he said anyone who taught contrary to it would be cursed (see Galatians 1:8). Before we can share the gospel with others, understanding its meaning is something we must get right. Our eternities, and the eternities of all our loved ones, depend on us getting it right.[2]

GOSPEL —
the message concerning Christ, the kingdom of God, and salvation

THE GOSPEL IS AN ANNOUNCEMENT

The word *gospel—euangelion—*was used in ancient Greece to signify an announcement of good news. Say, for example, a Greek general had defeated an invading army. He would send out a "gospel," declaring to all the citizens of the region that he had won the battle. He wasn't asking them to come and help but declaring to them his victory. No longer did they need to fear; they were free from danger.*

31 percent of all adults know the meaning of the expression "the gospel," according to Barna Research.

The gospel of Jesus is the announcement that Jesus is Lord and has won a great victory on our behalf. The gospel is not a command that we should do better so that God will accept us, but the announcement that Jesus has paid the full penalty for our sin. No longer do we need to live in fear. The battle has been won on our behalf—we need only to believe and receive it.

The gospel, as Tim Keller says, is not "good advice," but "good news." It's not primarily about what we must "do" but what Jesus has "done."[3]

---

* Facilitator: How do you define the gospel? On what is your definition based?

Understanding the "do/done" distinctive is perhaps the most important and counter-intuitive aspect of the gospel. While we'll dive into that a little more, first, let's consider why we need the gospel.

BAD NEWS AND THEN GOOD NEWS

An announcement of victory only makes sense in the context of battle; but far too many people are unaware that a battle even needed to be fought. It may be a nice gesture that Jesus *did* something for us, but why is it that Jesus had to *do* anything at all? We understand why we should believe in God, but why do we need Jesus and the cross?

The answer, distasteful as we often find it, is our sin.

The gospel is bad news before it is good news: Our sin had left us under a curse, death. We tend to think of our sin as not *that* bad—just mistakes, white lies, or indiscretions. The Bible says the opposite: Our sin makes us worthy of eternal condemnation. The apostle Paul says that we're "children under wrath," sons and daughter of disobedience (Ephesians 2:3). We've committed cosmic treason against our Creator, telling Him we'd rather be in charge of our own lives than let Him rule. Sin is the great "I" problem, when we focus more on ourselves and our desires than on God's perfect plan.*

The just punishment for our sin is death. God is a holy God, and sin is an offense and a corruption. Imagine how you might react to a blood transfusion that you learned had two to three molecules of the AIDS virus in it. It wouldn't matter that the amount was microscopic; even a little pollutes the entire vial. God is so holy and good that sin can't endure in His presence. To stand before God with sin on your record would be like a tissue paper touching the surface of the sun. It must be removed.

> "Your eyes are too pure to look on evil, and You cannot tolerate wrongdoing. So why do You tolerate those who are treacherous? Why are You silent while one who is wicked swallows up one who is more righteous than himself" (Habakkuk 1:13).

---

* Facilitator: Do you find it difficult to talk about sin with your peers? Why? Why is it important in light of the gospel to talk about sin?

Habakkuk explained God's pure goodness. How do you reconcile the fact that we all need Christ's reconciliation—no matter how righteous or wicked we think we are?

So the gospel begins as bad news, but thank God it doesn't end there. The gospel is the *good* news that Jesus put away our sin forever by His death on the cross. As Tim Keller says, even though we were so bad that Jesus had to die for our sin, He was so loving that He was glad to die for it.

THE GOSPEL IS GIFT-RIGHTEOUSNESS

Just about every religion in the world teaches us that God's approval of us is based upon how well we obey His laws. If we do enough, we can overcome the penalty of our sin and earn our place in heaven. The gospel turns that thinking on its head. Acceptance before God, which the Bible calls "righteousness," is given to us as a gift, purchased for us by Christ.

How do you think God feels about you right now? How do you determine that?

GRACE — Undeserved acceptance and love received from another, especially the characteristic attitude of God in providing salvation for sinners. In Christ Jesus, God's grace is open to all people, but the experience of God's grace is conditional upon human response.

Did you base your answer on what kind of week you've had? How consistent your quiet times have been? Whether you've been nice to your family or friends? Whether you kicked the dog? For many years qualifications like these drove my own response.

If I had a good week—a real "Christian" week—I felt close to God. When Sunday came around, I would feel like lifting my head and hands in worship, almost as if to say, "God, here I am! I just know that You're excited about seeing me this week." If I had a stellar week, I loved being in God's presence and was sure God was pretty stoked about having me there, too.

---

* Facilitator: Jewish tradition upholds that there are 613 commandments in the Torah, or the first five books of the Bible. Is it humanly possible to follow all of those every day? Do you believe that's what God expects of us? Explain why or why not.

But the opposite was also true. If I had done a poor job at being a *real* Christian, I felt pretty distant from God. If I had fallen to some temptations, been a jerk to my wife, dodged some easy opportunities to share Christ, was stingy with my money, had forgotten to recycle—on *those* weeks I felt like God wanted nothing to do with me. When I came to church, I had no desire to lift my soul up to God. I was pretty sure He wasn't thrilled to see me either. I could feel His displeasure—His lack of approval.

Why? Because in that moment I wasn't believing the gospel. Or, at least, I had forgotten it.

Think of a time when you offered grace to someone who wronged you or someone you cared for. How does that experience affect your view of God's gift of grace to you?*

The gospel is the news that Christ has suffered the full wrath of God for my sin. Jesus Christ traded places with me, living the perfect life I should have lived, and dying the death I had been condemned to die. In fact, 2 Corinthians 5 says that He actually *became* my sin so that I could literally become His righteousness:

> **"He made the One who did not know sin to be sin for us, so that we might become the righteousness of God in Him" (v. 21).**

---

* Facilitator: In what ways do you feel you have to prove yourself to God?

THE RESURRECTION (LUKE 24:5)

Resurrection is the central fact on which Christianity and the church are built and unique from all that went before it. Some Old Testament heroes of the faith were taken to heaven without enduring death— Enoch (Genesis 5:24) and Elijah (2 Kings 2:11). Jesus raised people from the dead (such as the son of the widow of Nain as well as Lazarus). These would die again. Jesus died. He was buried and stayed in the tomb three days. Then He came out of the empty tomb alive, never to enter a tomb again. The resurrected Christ was then taken to heaven to rule with God forever.

Other religions and people without religion may claim to believe in a life after death. Without Jesus, however, they have no evidence for their belief, no reason for their hope. The historical example of Jesus Christ proves that the God and Father of Jesus Christ has power over sin, death, and the grave. The historical promise of Jesus means that each of His followers can expect to participate in the resurrection of the dead and the rewards of Christ. A person who doesn't believe in Christ, who doesn't take up his cross, deny himself, and follow Jesus has not received Christ's promises and cannot expect to join Him in the rewards of eternal life after death.

Theologians call this "the great exchange." He took my record, died for it, and offers me His perfect record in return. He took my shameful nakedness and offers to clothe me with His righteousness. When I receive Him in repentance and faith, full acceptance becomes mine. Jesus Christ lived in my place, and died in my place, and then offered righteousness to me as a gift. Theologians call that "gift-righteousness."

To me, this means that God couldn't love me any more than He does right now, because God couldn't love and accept Christ any more than He does right now—and I am in Christ. God's righteousness has been given to me as a gift. He now sees me according to how Christ lived, not on the basis of what kind of week I have lived. Christ's salvation is 100 percent complete, and 100 percent the possession of those who have received it in repentance and faith.

Just let that sink in for a moment. Right now, if we're in Christ, when God looks at us—regardless of our situations—He sees the righteousness of Christ. If we really believed that, not only with our heads but also with our hearts, it would change everything in our lives.

Have you ever had the sense there was always just one more thing to do to get the "spiritual life thing" right? What's that one thing for you?

Do you ever feel He is judging your performance—that He'll love you more if you do better? Explain.*

Imagine if you could say this to God: *God, here is why I think You should hear my prayer: This week, I concluded a 40-day fast, and during that time I met Satan in the flesh, stared him down, and resisted all his temptations. And then I suffered unjustly at the hand of sinners, but did so without complaint or the first flash of selfish anger. The only time I opened my mouth was to forgive those who were doing that to me. Also, I walked on water, raised a few dead people, and fed 5,000 hungry men with a Hebrew Happy Meal.*

---

* Facilitator: Do you maintain other relationships in your life in which you feel like you always have to justify that you deserve to be in the relationship? How would you describe God's perspective on that kind of relationship?

According to the gospel, that's exactly what you can, and should, say.

Jesus' death has paid for every ounce of your sin; His perfect life has now been credited to you. In light of that, do you really feel like you could make God more favorable to you by doing your quiet time every day? Christ's obedience is so spectacular that there's nothing we could do to add to it, His death so final that nothing could take away from it.

Scripture says that we're not to come into the presence of God timidly or apprehensively but boldly:

> **"Therefore let us approach the throne of grace with boldness, so that we may receive mercy and find grace to help us at the proper time" (Hebrews 4:16).**

We can only approach God with boldness when we know that He sees us according to the accomplishments of Christ.

For most of us, this is completely counter-intuitive.

Martin Luther said that our hearts are hard-wired for "works-righteousness"—that is, the idea that our worth and approval by God fluctuate based on our performance. (See "Grace vs. Works" sidebar.) Unless we're actively preaching the gospel to ourselves daily, we've probably fallen back into "works-righteousness." We come by it naturally.*

In your theology, what's the relationship between what you believe and what you do?

GRACE VS. WORKS

"Paul diligently sets out in [Galatians] to teach us, to comfort us, and to keep us constantly aware of this great Christian righteousness. For if the truth of our being justified by Christ alone is lost, then all Christian truths are lost. There is no middle ground between 'passive' and 'works' righteousness. The person who wanders away from 'passive' righteousness has no other choice but live by 'works' righteousness. If he does not depend on the work of Christ, he must depend on his own work. So we must teach and continually repeat the truth of this 'passive' or 'Christian' righteousness so that Christians continue to hold to it and never confuse it with 'works' righteousness. On this truth, the church is built and has its being."

—Adapted from Martin Luther's commentary on Galatians[4]

---

* Facilitator: In what areas of your life are you timidly considering God's input?

"IT IS FINISHED!"

Just before His death on the cross, Jesus uttered a single word of victory: *tetelestai,* meaning "It is finished!" The verb *teleo* is related to several other Greek words that refer to something being finished, accomplished, completed, or coming to an end. The perfect tense of the Greek verb Jesus used indicates that He understood His death at this point in time to have abiding or lasting results. Jesus' death on the cross on our behalf was His purpose for coming into the world.[5]

How would you describe a person who lives consistently in the truth that Jesus' love for him or her precedes anything he or she might do to earn it?

The idea of gift-righteousness can be summarized in just four words: *Jesus in my place.* Jesus took our sin, suffering the full weight of its penalty. In return He offers us His righteousness. When we're united to Christ, what is ours becomes His and what is His becomes ours. Because Jesus, who deserved *commendation,* received *condemnation* instead, we who deserve condemnation can receive His commendation.

In Jesus' final moments on the cross, He said, "It is finished" (John 19:30). He was talking about the work of our salvation—He had done everything necessary to save us from our sin. There was nothing more that needed to be done. We need only to receive it.

What makes a gift special?

Jesus' death was a gift to humanity. Why do we so often struggle to see His death as our gift?

---

* Facilitator: Do you know someone who seems to always be seeking others' approval? How does that affect your relationship with them? Do you know someone who you sense is always seeking God's approval? How does that seem to affect their relationship with God?

HOW DO WE RECEIVE THE GIFT OF THE GOSPEL?

The gospel is a gift, and like any other gift, it must be received. So how do you receive the gospel? A terrified jailor once asked the apostle Paul a similar question:

> "Sirs, what must I do to be saved?" (Acts 16:30).

Paul's answer was simple:

> "Believe on the Lord Jesus, and you will be saved—you and your household" (Acts 16:31).

Believe means more than giving cognitive assent to a set of facts. *Believe* means "to rest your whole weight upon." We must not only believe that Jesus is the Lord; we must submit our lives to Him. We must not only believe that He has finished the work of our salvation; we must rest all our hopes for heaven on Him. This is what the Bible means by "*believe* on the Lord Jesus."

Think of it like sitting down in a chair. You might believe that a chair can hold the weight of your body, but you're not "believing in" the chair until you transfer your weight from your legs onto the chair. You can talk all you like about the power of the chair to support you, but until your weight is actually resting on the chair, your "belief" is just bluster.

> **BIBLICAL POSTURES OF WORSHIP AND PRAYER**
> - Standing (Mark 11:25)
> - Kneeling (Daniel 6:10)
> - Prostrate on one's face (Joshua 5:14)
> - Praying aloud (Psalm 55:17)
> - Bowed heads (Exodus 4:31)
> - Eyes looking heavenward (Acts 7:55)

Conversion to Christ is just like that. It's not merely accepting a set of facts and declaring them to be true. It's assuming a *posture* of repentance and faith toward the finished work of Christ.

What does a posture of repentance and faith look like on a daily basis?

Conversion isn't a ceremony you go through or a prayer you pray. Conversion is simply believing that Jesus is Lord and submitting to Him, believing that He has finished the work of your salvation and resting your hopes for heaven on it. It's "sitting down" in "the chair" of His Lordship and His finished work.

We call the act of submitting to Jesus as Lord "repentance." *Repentance* literally means "changing your mind" about something, so to repent of your sin means to "change your mind" about who is in charge of your life. Repentance is not resolving to do a little better—to go to church more, to feel worse for your sins, to be more moral. When you repent, you surrender every part of your life to His control.

While repentance may lead God to forgive, it's not our repentance that restores the relationship. It's because we're forgiven that He starts this relationship with us anew. Like C.S. Lewis used to say, "We do not come to God as bad people trying to become good people; we come as rebels to lay down our arms."[6]

We call the act of resting your hopes for heaven on the cross "faith." Faith in Jesus isn't trying to do better or turning over a new leaf. Faith is believing that He has done everything necessary to save you and resting all your hopes on His finished work.

When I say to someone, "Are you a Christian?" the most common answer I get back is something like, "Well, I'm trying. I'm doing my best. Better now than I used to be. I'm going to church more now and trying to obey the commandments better." Sadly, that shows they still don't get the gospel at all. They still think "Christian" is a title that they earn.

A true Christian is one who recognizes that they could never earn that title; Jesus earned it in our place and gave it to us as a gift. We're accepted before God not because of what we do but because of what He has done.

When someone asks me if I know for sure if I will go to heaven when I die, I say, *Absolutely. Jesus was my substitute, which means I no longer depend on how "righteous" I am to gain entrance into heaven. I rest in what He accomplished for me. We traded places. I am as sure of heaven as He is. He has become my salvation.*

Does that sound too good to be true? If so, then you're probably getting it. The sign that you've understood the gospel is that you're filled with humility because of how little you deserve eternal life, and filled with wonder at how good God is to give it to you.

What's the difference between humility and confidence in the Lord? How do you determine the right balance?

THE CLEAREST GOSPEL VERSE IN THE BIBLE

Perhaps the clearest, most concise explanation of this is given in Paul's gospel summary in Romans 4:

> **"But to the one who does not work, but believes on Him who declares the ungodly to be righteous, his faith is credited for righteousness" (v. 5).**

That verse has three very important phrases:

"But to the one who does not work..."
That is, to the one who realizes that there's nothing they could ever do to earn eternal life

"...but believes on Him who declares the ungodly to be righteous..."
The one who believes that God did the work necessary to save Him, just like God said He did.

"...his faith is credited for righteousness."
God counts that belief, that faith, as righteousness to us. Paul compares our belief in Christ to Abraham's belief in God's promise to give him a son. Though he was nearly 100 years old, Abraham chose to believe God could bring a child from a dead womb, and God "credited to him for righteousness" (Romans 4:3).

In what area of your life do you need to take a lesson from Abraham and focus not on "working" but on "believing"?

The moment we repentantly believe God brought back the lifeless body of Jesus from the deadness of the tomb, after His offering as a payment for our sin, we are declared similarly righteous.

> **"If you confess with your mouth, 'Jesus is Lord,' and believe in your heart that God raised Him from the dead, you will be saved" (Romans 10:9).**

Righteousness is a free gift to all who believe that God is gracious enough to give it to them in Christ.

Have you ever personally received that gift? If not, what's stopping you from doing so right now?

Understanding the gospel leads to a profound life change—not just of your behavior but of your heart. As you see the glory of the God who has forgiven you, and experience the beauties of His grace, you'll find that your heart begins to desire Him more than sin.

THE GOSPEL ISN'T JUST THE DIVING BOARD

The gospel isn't just the "beginning point" of Christianity, a prayer you pray to begin your Christian life, or the diving board off of which you jump into the pool of Christianity. The gospel *is* the pool in which you swim, day by day. Once you've believe the gospel, the way you grow in Christ is by going deeper into the gospel. You become more aware of how gracious He is and how incredible is the gift He has given you in Christ.

Jesus told us to "abide" in Him daily.

"Abide in Me, and I in you. As the branch cannot bear fruit of itself unless it abides in the vine, so neither can you unless you abide in Me. I am the vine, you are the branches; he who abides in Me and I in him, he bears much fruit, for apart from Me you can do nothing. If anyone does not abide in Me, he is thrown away as a branch and dries up; and they gather them, and cast them into the fire and they are burned. If you abide in Me, and My words abide in you, ask whatever you wish, and it will be done for you. My Father is glorified by this, that you bear much fruit, and so prove to be My disciples. Just as the Father has loved Me, I have also loved you; abide in My love. If you keep My commandments, you will abide in My love; just as I have kept My Father's commandments and abide in His love" (John 15:4-10, NASB).

Abiding in Christ means reminding ourselves constantly there's nothing we could ever do that would make God love us more, and nothing we've done that makes Him love us less.

Literally, nothing at all.

What about if you gave away all your money, would He not love you just a little bit more? *Nope.*

What if you sold everything and went to live on the foreign mission field? *No again.*

What if you finally began to treat the people you love with grace? *Nada.*

What if you took out the trash for your mom like she asked? *She might love you more, but God wouldn't.*

JESUS LIVES IN US

No matter our circumstances, we're not alone in life. How is this possible? Because as believers in Christ, we have a personal relationship with Him, and He promises to be with us always. John 15:1-5 helps us understand our relationship with Jesus more clearly.

Florists know the importance of staying connected to the vine. Freshly cut flowers stay fresh and beautiful for only a few days. Once the flowers are cut off from their roots in the ground, they begin to droop. Apart from the vine, they'll die. No profit can be had from detached, wilted flowers.

This is the symbolism Jesus used in John 15 to describe our (the branches) connection to Him (the vine). According to this passage, we're incapable of living a life that glorifies God and embraces His grace apart from a growing relationship with Jesus.

Investing in our relationship with Jesus should be of primary importance. We're to glorify Him, yield to Him, and love and serve others in His name. Strengthening this relationship has a direct effect on the quality of the rest of our relationships. We don't produce fruit by being high-achieving, motivated, super-productive makers of fruit, but by yielding to God, the vinedresser. When we submit and lean into God—abide in Him—He enables us to bear fruit.[8]

What if you went one full week without a single, lustful thought? *God's acceptance of you is based on the fact that Christ went a lifetime without sinning against Him in even the slightest way. Now you are in Him and He is in you. Thus, God could not love you more than He does right now because He loves Christ perfectly.*

You must dwell on this great truth *daily*. Sometimes hourly. Sometimes every minute. It's the only way to drive out fear, unbelief, and temptation.

Why so often? Remember, you're hard-wired for works-righteousness. When you're not deliberately thinking about the gospel, you have probably slid back into self-justification. It's a lot like the plastic rodents in that "whack-a-mole" game you play at the fair. Just when you knock one down, another appears from a different place. The moment we take our eyes off of the gospel, those rodents of self-righteousness and self-condemnation spring back up. So we must pound them with the counter-intuitive truth of the gospel: God's acceptance is given to us in its entirety as a gift we receive by faith, to the praise and glory of God.

List the things you've done today—the good and the bad. Why isn't God's love for us dependent on what we do?

Do you believe Jesus loves you even before you follow Him? Explain.

At our church, I encourage people to pray this phrase back to God every day as a reminder that there's nothing they need to do to gain God's approval, but that it's theirs as a gift in Christ:

"In Christ, there is nothing I can do that would make You love me more; nothing I have done that makes You love me less."*

---

* Facilitator: What would change if we saw ourselves, first and foremost, as those sent by God on His mission?

I encourage you to pray this back to God every day for at least a month, until it gets into your bloodstream and so saturates your thinking that you see everything with gospel-vision. Nothing in your life will ever be the same.

THE DAILY WALK

Once you've decided to follow Christ and claim His love and grace over your life, you have eternal life in Him:

> **"A thief comes only to steal and to kill and to destroy. I have come so that they may have life and have it in abundance" (John 10:10).**

God wants us to have life "in abundance" in Him. That's exactly why He's given us the indwelling Holy Spirit. Through Him, we have God's power living inside of us.

> **"I will ask the Father, and He will give you another Counselor to be with you forever. He is the Spirit of truth. The world is unable to receive Him because it doesn't see Him or know Him. But you do know Him, because He remains with you and will be in you" (John 14:16-17).**

What evidence shows that you have received the Holy Spirit's power?*

YOUR SPIRITUAL TRAINING ROOM

One way to stay spiritually healthy is to spend time in daily Bible reading and prayer. Just like in physical training, getting started is the hardest part. Here are some steps toward a daily training regimen:

- Find a place to serve as your spiritual training room.
- Establish a regular time, as best you can. Most of us do better in a routine. But rotating the time is better than no time.
- Gather your training equipment (Bible, a notebook to record thoughts and impressions, and even some of your favorite Christian music).
- Consider adding a devotional guide for structure to your Bible reading.
- Read and meditate on the Scripture and journal your thoughts.
- Pray for insight while reading, offer praise to God, confess sins, and make requests to the Lord. Conclude by listening for the Lord to speak to you.

This is only one step to growing in godliness. Participation in corporate worship, small group Bible study, discipleship groups, and church or community service opportunities also enhance your spiritual growth.

---

* Facilitator: How might we work together to move from an emphasis on once-a-week worship to focusing on a supernatural, daily walk with Christ? How might this affect our ability to share the gospel with others?

God puts His Spirit within the hearts of believers to mark them as His own. Paul used the imagery of the seal, which would've brought to his readers' mind Caesar's ring, as a sign of a royal covenant (see Ephesians 1:13; 4:30). Being sealed was a mark of security, ownership, and authentication. It's a teaser and a taste of the incredible inheritance all Christians have coming. And that's not an inheritance anyone wants to miss out on. In short, once we trust in Christ and become Christians, we're in the grasp of God—and no one can change that.

Does knowing that you're "in Christ" make any practical difference in the way you make decisions about your future?

As a Christian, what responsibilities do you have to Christ? What duties might need more of your attention?

As Christians, we have a massive task—sharing the gospel of Jesus Christ with the world. This is quite an impossible task without the help of God's power, His Holy Spirit, dwelling in us. Yet we are not alone. In Acts 1:8, Jesus promised the power of the Holy Spirit to carry out the mission. God doesn't need us for this mission, but He wants us to experience the overwhelming joy that comes through partnering with Him. As the body working together, we will accomplish the mission of God when the love of Christ so fully engulfs our hearts that sharing the gospel and loving others as Christ loved us become the natural expressions of our relationship with God. Only by the Holy Spirit's power will we do this.

In what areas of your life do you want to experience more of the Holy Spirit's power? What do you think is your part in having that happen?

How is the Holy Spirit changing how you think, what you value, and the way you live?

THIS WEEK REFLECT ON . . .

> GROWING WITH GOD
- Spend some time re-examining exactly what you would call "the gospel."
- Take an opportunity to thank those in your life who have modeled God's standard and what daily living out the gospel looks like. Write them a quick message letting them know how much you appreciate their dedication to sharing the message of Christ with others.
- Make a list of what you've repented from. Then, shred or destroy the list, remembering that it's been offered to God. He's able and willing to forgive.

> MAKING A CHANGE
- Practice abiding in Christ this week. Dwell in God's Word. Meditate on Scripture, chewing on it and savoring it. This doesn't come easily at first, but the more we do it, the more natural it feels. After a while, we will feel Scripture shaping us and we will naturally begin to live its message.
- Make a genuine effort to grow closer to God. He desires to be close to you. As you implement these three shifts in your approach, you'll find your time with Jesus sweeter, enduring, and fruitful.

> FURTHER STUDY
- For an in-depth look at Paul and Timothy's emphasis on being loyal to the gospel and teaching it to others, check out *Mentor* by Chuck Lawless (available at *threadsmedia.com*).
- For an interesting perspective on how the story of the gospel can be seen even from the beginning of Scripture, check out *Creation Unraveled: The Gospel According to Genesis* by Matt Carter and Halim Suh (also available at *threadsmedia.com*).

Why should I share the gospel?

by Rob Turner

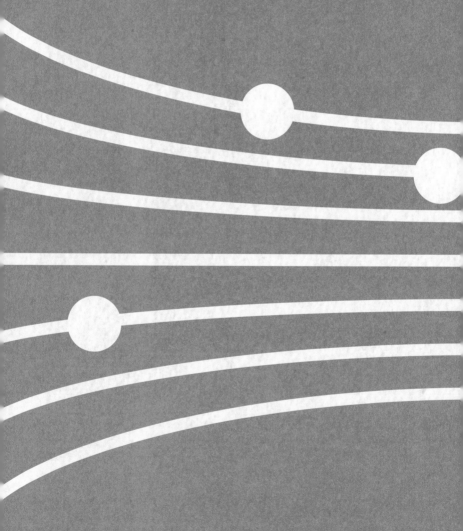

"If he have faith, the believer cannot be restrained. He betrays himself. He breaks out. He confesses and teaches this gospel to the people at the risk of life itself."
—Martin Luther,
Preface to the New Testament[1]

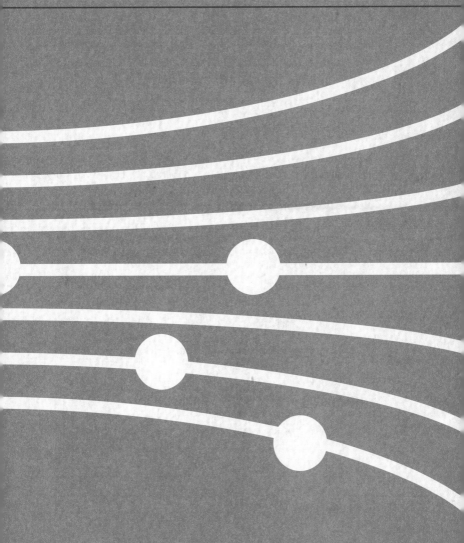

Sharing the good news of Jesus in certain parts of the world is indeed a dangerous thing. Persecution of Christians is alive and well in places like Cambodia, Saudi Arabia, North Korea, and Sudan. That's but a short list of countries where the oppression or outright suppression of Christians is all too real. Cultural isolation, severed ties from family, or outright physical death are continual story lines that play out in many of these unreached contexts. Some of those story lines we hear through our multi-layered streams of media, but others occur in stark silence.

For every martyr with a known name, such as Stephen in Acts 6, there are many who are nameless. The saints in Hebrews 11 experienced suffering and death simply because they were desiring a "better place" that's continually ruled by a powerful and gracious King (v. 16).

Yet there's another place we often overlook that's overtly hostile to the gospel: our own hearts.

TAKE IT TO HEART

Our hearts are the seats of our motivations and our wills and therefore lock us into our daily and overall life directions. Unfortunately, our hearts can be pretty messy places. Scripture says so.

> **"The heart is more deceitful than anything else, and incurable—who can understand it?" (Jeremiah 17:9).**

Our hearts give birth to vices such as lust, hatred, anger, and harmful words (Leviticus 19:17; Psalm 66:18; 101:5; James 1:26). This is why Solomon, who definitely didn't heed the Spirit's counsel, exhorts his readers:

> **"Guard your heart above all else, for it is the source of life"**
> **(Proverbs 4:23).**

MEMORY VERSES
Psalm 51:10; 73:26
Proverbs 3:5-6
Philippians 4:6-7

To state it succinctly, what's inside of our hearts gushes out and compels us to action. This is why our hearts—or more specifically, our desires—can create significant barriers between our knowledge of our redemption through Christ and the active proclaiming of that redemption to others. We have to admit as disciples of Jesus that we never lack reasons to proclaim Him to others.

Are *all* Christians called to share the gospel? Why or why not?*

If we're commanded to tell the story of Jesus to others, what keeps us from accomplishing the task?

Evangelism is the fundamental catalyst to spread Christ-exalted worship throughout the world.

> "But how can they call on Him they have not believed in? And how can they believe without hearing about Him? And how can they hear without a preacher? And how can they preach unless they are sent? As it is written: How beautiful are the feet of those who announce the gospel of good things! But all did not obey the gospel. For Isaiah says, Lord, who has believed our message?" (Romans 10:14-16).

"His voice leads us not into timid discipleship but into bold witness."
—Charles Stanley

And evangelism will seemingly usher in the second coming of Christ Himself when His good news is heard in all the nations and people groups.

> "This good news of the kingdom will be proclaimed in all the world as a testimony to all nations. And then the end will come" (Matthew 24:14).

In spite of these reasons many professing Christians do little or no personal evangelism and struggle with significant fear in sharing their faith.

I teach a class on personal evangelism at a Christian university, and there are "usual suspects" of fear that emerge within our class lectures.

---

* Facilitator: Discuss the benefits gained from sharing the gospel—both personally and in the lives of others.

Believers today don't have the same proofs Jesus' followers had on resurrection Sunday. We can't hear His voice, examine His scars, eat with Him, or listen as He explains the Scriptures. Nonbelievers and believers alike may sometimes wonder if Jesus' resurrection really occurred. We still have proof today that Christ is alive. We know He has changed our lives and the lives of others. We feel His presence in our lives. We hear His voice through the Bible. Although belief in Jesus always requires a step of faith, enough evidence exists that we can let go of our doubts and accept the wondrous reality of Jesus' resurrection.

The fears of giving wrong or confusing information, the perceived inability to respond to questions, coming across as a certain stereotype ("unloving Bible thumper!"), and outright personal rejection stop many a disciple in his or her tracks from speaking Christ to others. In this postmodern age where it's in vogue to question and deconstruct every claim of truth, a growing fear within twentysomething Christians rises out of a latent agnosticism over one's own conversion or the content of the gospel itself. Boldness to proclaim rarely grows in the garden of doubt or cynicism.

How would our lives be different if we let go of all our doubts? Why is doubtless living hopeful living?

FEAR'S NEMESIS

What then is the antidote to our fears and weak desires of communicating the most important news in the universe? The answer is in a small ancient letter written to a cluster of anxious believers in Jesus who were facing tremendous trials, both inward and outward. John, the disciple "whom Jesus loved" exhorted these vulnerable believers by reminding them, "There is no fear in love; instead, perfect love drives out fear" (1 John 4:18a). Only love that is God-created, displayed through the redemption of Christ, and empowered by His Spirit has the propulsive power to extinguish our fears, no matter what they may be.

Here is good news. We already have a natural desire to communicate who or what we love. Have you ever noticed how we naturally offer a running commentary of such things as song lyrics, T.V. or movie scripts, statistics on our favorite athletes or teams, or one-liners off Twitter accounts and Facebook feeds? We simply can't help but immerse our attention into those things and consequently share them with others. To speak of what we love is seemingly hard wired into our human DNA.

C. S. Lewis, in his study on the Psalms, noticed a dynamic that expresses this idea much better than I'm able:

> "We delight to praise what we enjoy because the praise not merely expresses but completes the enjoyment; it is its appointed consummation. It is not out of compliment that lovers keep on telling one another how beautiful they are; the delight is incomplete till it is expressed."[2]

The last line is an important one: "the delight is incomplete till it is expressed." Our lack of personal evangelism isn't because we can't arrive at a precise definition of "the gospel" or that we lack the needed resources to do personal evangelism.

Our lack of evangelism is directly tied to one thing: Our failure to see Jesus as our greatest delight and the ultimate lover of our souls. We will rarely "do" the Great Commission (Matthew 28:18-20) when we don't practice the Great Commandment (Matthew 22:36-40). Loving God and loving others is the fuel that propels the proclaiming of the gospel and the making of disciples.

Read Matthew 22:36-40. How is loving God related to loving people?*

Let's look now at how the church helps us fulfill both the Great Commandment and the Great Commission.

OVERCOMING FEAR IN SHARING THE GOSPEL

It's easy to focus on how someone might respond. It's also easy to forget how much people need the Lord and how much Christ desires a relationship with lost persons. So how are we to respond to our own fears?

• Recognize that fear is natural, although we're seeking to live in the power of the supernatural.

• Recognize that fear isn't from God but a tool of Satan. We do battle against the forces of hell when we share our faith.

• Love will disperse fear. John wrote, "There is no fear in love; instead, perfect love drives out fear, because fear involves punishment. So the one who fears has not reached perfection in love" (1 John 4:18).

• Fear should drive us to a greater dependence on God. Evangelism is about God, who chooses to use us. We are never stronger than when we have bowed our spirits in dependence upon God to do what we cannot.

• Fear should increase our desire to become more skilled in sharing Christ.

• Fear can be used to drive us to develop sensitivities and skills in sharing the greatest story ever told.[3]

---

* Facilitator: Make a list of challenging situations in which to spread the gospel. Which of these situations challenges you the most in your attempts to spread the gospel? Why are these situations intimidating? How can you overcome this fear?

TOGETHER WE HAVE PURPOSE

Through the church we learn how to love others, by seeing Christ modeled through the loving actions of other Christians. And it's through the church that non-Christians see God clearly and are drawn to Him.

> "'But you,' He asked them, 'who do you say that I am?' Simon Peter answered, 'You are the Messiah, the Son of the living God!' And Jesus responded, 'Simon son of Jonah, you are blessed because flesh and blood did not reveal this to you, but My Father in heaven. And I also say to you that you are Peter, and on this rock I will build My church, and the forces of Hades will not overpower it. I will give you the keys of the kingdom of heaven, and whatever you bind on earth is already bound in heaven, and whatever you loose on earth is already loosed in heaven" (Matthew 16:15-19).

What do you think Jesus meant when He said "on this rock I will build My church" (v. 18)?

Verse 18 includes the first use of the Greek word *ekklesia,* translated "church." *Ekklesia* refers to an assembly of people called out for a particular purpose. When Jesus introduced this concept to the disciples, He declared that He was creating a new group of people to represent Him in the world until His kingdom is established on earth.

Why is the church important? What is the church called to do?

What can you do to help support the mission of the church?

CALLED TO GO

Besides being essential for our growth in Christ (see Philemon 1:6), evangelism is a sacred command from our Lord. All people are called collectively (through the church) and individually to honor this command.

Matthew 28:18-20 records the Great Commission, one of the most commonly referenced passages of Scripture.

> "Then Jesus came near and said to them, 'All authority has been given to Me in heaven and on earth. Go, therefore, and make disciples of all nations, baptizing them in the name of the Father and of the Son and of the Holy Spirit, teaching them to observe everything I have commanded you. And remember, I am with you always, to the end of the age" (Matthew 28:18-20).

For many Christians, the Great Commission is more aptly thought of as the Great Omission. We'd rather not discuss our faith with others—it's scary and unfamiliar work—so we leave that part out of our obedience to God and focus on personal growth and making disciples. But sharing the gospel with others isn't an option; it's a critical component of passing on the faith and introducing other people to Jesus.

Because evangelism can be so intimidating, we often overlook another detail included in the Great Commission: the daunting task of making disciples of all nations isn't intended to be done on our own.

First, Jesus tells us that He now has all authority on earth and heaven, then He tells us to go and make disciples, and then He says He'll always be with us. Catch anything in that order? First, He can do anything. Second, He's given us a job to do. Third, He'll be with us, so don't sweat it and don't skip it. Help is always with us, and this Help can do anything in heaven or earth. This truth can eradicate any of the fears we have regarding evangelism. Believe it, and be a part of the purpose He's given His church.

In your own words, what is the Great Commission?

What are you doing to fulfill this Commission?*

How can knowing that Christ remains with you help in this?

---

* Facilitator: Commit together to taking the Great Commission seriously. As a group, commit to 1) Doing group evangelism once a month, 2) Bringing one new person into the group within the next six months, and 3) Having older members mentor the younger/newer ones.

The world needs to know who Jesus really is and what the benefits are of putting faith in Him. Jesus gave us the responsibility to make those truths known. The potential impact of obedience to that calling is world-changing.

Why is it important for every believer to get involved in the Great Commission? What happens when you don't own your part of the effort?

Go. Make disciples. Baptize them. Teach them. Remember His presence. In which of these five areas are you most involved?*

In which area would you like to get more involved?

The Great Commission reminds us that we truly can reach the world for Christ. This is the desired impact of the church. But to have that worldwide impact, we must first acknowledge that the world needs to know who Jesus is and commit to telling them. If we do this, not only will our personal faith grow, but the Christian faith will expand around the world.

LIVING IN THE MEANTIME

It's easy to get caught up in the present, giving little thought to the afterlife. Everything in our culture trains us to think this way. Plus, the longer the wait for Jesus' second coming, the less we anticipate His return during our lifetime. So how do we balance the demands of this world (like school debt, car trouble, illness, rent, family dysfunction, etc.) with the hope and anticipation we should have in Jesus' return?

There is one undeniable, inexorable fact: Jesus will return. What does it mean to be ready for His return and to remain faithful to Him? How we respond to this truth will determine how we live and what kind of impact we have here on earth.

> "Look! I am coming quickly, and My reward is with Me to repay each person according to what he has done. I am the Alpha and the Omega, the First and the Last, the Beginning

---

* **Facilitator:** Take a minute to reflect upon the magnitude of the Great Commission. Discuss 1) what each command means, 2) how the church can follow, and 3) what role you personally have in obeying.

and the End. 'Blessed are those who wash their robes, so that they may have the right to the tree of life and may enter the city by the gates'" (Revelation 22:12-14).

How do you reconcile Jesus' statement with the fact that He has yet to return?

What might Jesus be trying to teach us in our waiting?

We can't know how long it will be until His return, but these few verses give us clues of how to live for Him in the meantime. First, our time on earth is limited, which means so are our opportunities to obey God, serve Him, love others, and make a difference in our world.

> "Therefore, whether we are at home or away, we make it our aim to be pleasing to Him. For we must all appear before the tribunal of Christ, so that each may be repaid for what he has done in the body, whether good or worthless. Therefore, because we know the fear of the Lord, we seek to persuade people. We are completely open before God, and I hope we are completely open to your consciences as well" (2 Corinthians 5:9-11).

What's the purpose of our good works? Are these "works" strictly external or do they also include our inner motivations?*

DON'T WALK AROUND HELL. The only reality that human beings are truly entitled to is hell. It's indeed a sobering joy that because of Christ His disciples will never experience an eternity separated from Him—an eternity that's described in the Bible with metaphors such as an "outer darkness" (Matthew 25:30), "eternal fire" (Matthew 25:41), an "abyss" (Luke 8:31), and a place of continual "torment" (Revelation 14:11). Jesus actually described hell more than He described heaven.

Unfortunately, because believers know that they aren't going to hell, they decide to get over hell. This is done by not revisiting on a consistent basis the doctrine of hell and walking around or glossing over the parts of Scripture that address it. Over time, our hearts for the lost—especially those people who are difficult for us to relate to—begin to become less merciful. We begin to view people from our own reference point instead of the reality of their tragic eternity: If they don't turn to Christ for redemption, they will literally go to hell.

---

* Facilitator: Many Christians hold up evangelism as the purest expression of faith. Other Christians believe social action is the key to showing love to the world. Is one right and the other wrong? Did God intend for these two things to be separated? Was Jesus more concerned with one than the other?

Second, anticipating Jesus' return gives us something to hope in through the ups and downs of life. Third, while we wait on Jesus, we get to play a part in making His name known and leading people to a relationship with Him.

Why is it significant that Jesus will return to the world?

What role does that play in keeping us focused on sharing the good news of Jesus Christ?

What are you doing to make the most of this wait?

HOW TO BE FAITHFUL

Let's spend some time now on the ways to protect your love for Christ and to continually "honor the Messiah as Lord in your hearts" (1 Peter 3:15a). The hope is that these methods would be effective in growing your enjoyment of Christ and that your love, then, consequently cascades into expressing Him. (Disclaimer: Please don't read these as a formula but rather as ways to dislodge our inordinate desires for lesser things than the sufficiency of Jesus.)

1. Stay Focused on God.

There's good reason why numerous books and social media commentaries are available on our need as Christians to see the gospel as our whole lives—not just as a baseline. As Tim Keller, pastor of Redeemer Presbyterian, has stated, "The gospel is not just the ABC's of Christianity, it is the A to Z of Christianity."[4]

Keller's words are a good reminder because we can often go through spiritual droughts of gospel amnesia. We shouldn't view the gospel as *only* something Jesus accomplished in history that we received in our past to obtain something for our future. Yes, the actual events of Jesus' coming as the promised Messiah, His perfect obedience to God's righteous standards, His perfect sacrifice through the cross, and His victorious resurrection did indeed occur in a particular time in human history. However, the power of the gospel is an ongoing present reality.

We not only need the gospel to cover our sinfulness and to guarantee a glorious eternity; we need the gospel for *everything*! From the most mundane activities of our day-to-day lives to the "big ticket item" decisions that pivot the trajectory of our lives—the gospel should infuse all of it.

This was the heart of the apostle Paul when he bluntly asserted to the church in ancient Rome that he was "not ashamed of the gospel, because it is God's power for salvation to everyone who believes" (Romans 1:16). Grammatically, this verse can read as the gospel being "the ongoing power of salvation."

What has changed about our mission as Christians since Jesus' original charge to the disciples?

In a typical day, what distracts you from staying focused on God's purposes?

In his letter to the church at Galatia, Paul wrote, "The life I now live in the body, I live by faith in the Son of God, who loved me and gave Himself for me" (Galatians 2:20).

SIX WAYS TO FOCUS ON GOD

1. **Seek out private worship.** Having a daily time of worship and Bible reading places you in the zone of the supernatural. Shoot for seven days a week but hit at least five. See what God begins to show you.

2. **Connect with a church member** who's in agreement with you to follow God and seek Him daily. Meet once a week with that friend.

3. **Make a difference in one person's life.** Pastor Andy Stanley says it like this: "Do for one what you wish you could do for everyone."

4. **Set boundaries** on frivolous spending and activities that disrupt your spiritual journey.

5. **Give up trying to control people.** Simply love them and work on yourself. It's amazing what happens when we allow people to experience the consequences of their actions. Instead of trying to "fix" people, just love them and let them see you live with integrity.

6. **Look for God's hand, and you'll be amazed!** There are miracles and unexplained mysteries all around us. once you find them, you'll bolster your faith to ask God for big things.[5]

Jerry Bridges, a popular and well respected author, summed up this important truth when he wrote,

"Paul lived every day by faith in the shed blood and righteousness of Christ. Every day he looked to Christ alone for his acceptance with the Father. He believed, like Peter (see 1 Peter 2:4-5), that even our best deeds—our spiritual sacrifices—are acceptable to God only through Jesus Christ. Perhaps no one apart from Jesus Himself has ever been as committed a disciple both in life and ministry as the apostle Paul. Yet he did not look to his own performance but to Christ's 'performance' as the sole basis of his acceptance with God."[6]

What do we learn about God from His desire to be known and to use us to make His name known?

2. Pray Urgently and Expectantly.

Throughout church history there has never been a genuine movement of people coming to faith in Christ without intentional prayer. Interestingly, on many "prayer lists" in churches people are on there for everything from cancer to someone's hangnail or a sick cat. (I promise I'm not making that up.) This isn't to say that God doesn't care about our physical needs, but isn't it important that people are being prayed for simply because they are lost without a shepherd? It seems our valuing of earthly comfort has eclipsed our deepest eternal need of Christ. If the need of Christ is that evident in us, then how much more vital is it in those who aren't Christians? We must prayerfully and urgently share the good news.

If you struggle with a heart to share the gospel, then start praying for a new one. The more we seek Christ in prayer the more we become sensitized to His heart, which is a shepherd's heart that would leave 99 sheep to go after one that was lost.* You can see this use of prayer as Paul asked the church in Colossae to pray:

---

* **Facilitator:** Discuss ways your group could help one another strengthen your hearts toward sharing the gospel in your area and around the world. What tangible steps can you take right now?

"Devote yourselves to prayer; stay alert in it with thanksgiving. At the same time, pray also for us that God may open a door to us for the message, to speak the mystery of the Messiah, for which I am in prison, so that I may reveal it as I am required to speak" (Colossians 4:2-4).

A crucial encouragement for us to pray is having the confidence that God is the Creator of the harvest and that prayer is the key to mobilizing workers to collect the harvest of redeemed people.

"After this, the Lord appointed 70 others, and He sent them ahead of Him in pairs to every town and place where He Himself was about to go. He told them: 'The harvest is abundant, but the workers are few. Therefore, pray to the Lord of the harvest to send out workers into His harvest'" (Luke 10:1-2).

It's a fearful thought that so few people carry the charge of bringing the good news of salvation to so many. That's why it's important to prayerfully remind ourselves that we're simply workers in His harvest. We just need to be faithful in our share of the work.

PHILIP: LEADING BY EXAMPLE

The New Testament makes it clear that every Christian should be an evangelist—one who shares the good news of Jesus Christ with others. Still, many Christians claim they don't know how to do so or leave that task up to others. Studying about Philip can help us learn about how we can live with the motivation to share the gospel. Read Acts 8:30-35. Philip's approach to evangelism included obeying God's leading, approaching people, asking questions, and presenting the gospel.

All around us are people who are lost and desperately in need of a relationship with Jesus. Rather than making excuses or adopting an attitude of unconcern or disbelief, Philip took decisive action and presented the gospel to those with whom he came into contact. We must do the same. God wants His children to spread the gospel everywhere they go.

What does it mean to live intentionally for Christ, day in and day out?*

3. Find Joy in the Journey.
Following Christ and spreading the word about Him isn't easy. The day-in, day-out can be difficult. So how can we carry joy with us?

---

* Facilitator: Like the two followers of Jesus on the road to Emmaus, what does the resurrected Jesus need to reveal or change in your life? Spiritual vision? Unbelief? Discouragement?

Do life with people who are bold for the gospel. If your core community languishes in mediocrity or are cultural only in their view of Christianity it will very difficult to be bold in proclaiming your faith.

For a biblical example of boldness, compare Peter in the Book of Acts with Peter in the Gospels. For all of his faith and love for Jesus, in the Gospels he's impulsive and often motivated by his emotions; Peter displayed fear and insecurity on the night he denied Jesus. In Acts, though, he's quite the opposite. His faith is mature, and he expertly leads the fledgling church with boldness through threats, imprisonments, and persecution. It's hard to believe we're reading about the same Peter.

Think about someone in your life who models Peter's boldness. What attributes enable that person to speak so boldly for Christ?

How can boldness be seen as an act of genuine love for others?

What would boldness in your faith require you to adopt or change about your current beliefs and actions?

Be obedient to God. Being a Christian is, at times, a walk of blind faith, and sometimes following God's will can be counter-intuitive. Through the days when obeying God's commands and loving others is extremely difficult, we're called to be persistent and obedient. It's easy to get bogged down with today's to-do list or focus on our anxiety—unanswered questions, financial uncertainty, effects of our decisions, and so forth. Yet through it all, God is showing us who He is and who we are meant to be. He is faithful, and He will use us when we choose to be obedient to Him.

When you feel His prompting, ignore the doubts, fears, and excuses. Be obedient to what He's asking you to do, and God will use your faithfulness to bring about His miraculous plan.

Why is it important that we be obedient to God's prompting? What's the difference between immediate and resistant obedience?

4. Let Joy Give You a Thick Skin.

The possible rejection or reprisal of your witness may be what God intends of your own growth in Him. We need Him to be like Him. We won't see our continual need for Him if we manage our life in such a way that avoids as much conflict and hardship as possible. While that may be true, rejection is never fun. To be rejected by someone, especially if that person is of significant value to us (parent, friend, dating relationship, spouse, etc.) stings.

On the other side of the coin, reprisal is equally hurtful. This occurs when anyone reacts in harmful ways to something we've said or done. The hurt is intensified when what we are saying or doing is for that person's ultimate good. The twin possibilities of rejection or reprisal thwart many an opportunity to communicate Jesus.

Interestingly, the New Testament provides us with a radical reorientation about hard reactions we may receive from exclaiming and living Christ among others. The Scriptures remind us that persecution, no matter the degree, is to be expected and is in fact an indication of our faith in Christ.*

Jesus said unequivocally that His disciples would be persecuted (John 15:18-21) and that the world will have hatred toward those who aren't of this world (John 17:14-18). The apostle Paul's consistent message to the early churches was that they must go through many hardships to enter the kingdom of God (Acts 14:22). This isn't legalism by which the journey of suffering for the gospel causes salvation but suffering is built upon our foundational joy in Christ.

PAUL'S GOSPEL

Paul took great pains in his efforts for evangelism. For him, the gospel was not just the good news of conversion; it was the good news of an entire way of life that led to everlasting benefits. Paul considered himself a partner in the good news, sharing in the blessings Christ gives to all who respond to Him in faith. First Corinthians 9:19-23 records Paul's account of how he accommodated his behavior to reach different groups of people for Christ. How does this accommodation relate to us? The answer is simple. We are to base our actions on what will lead others to become Christians. We are to do everything we can that is evangelistic. Consider for a moment the kinds of people who live within three miles of you. What can you do differently or better to adapt your outreach so that some of these people can be won to Christ?

---

* Facilitator: Commit as a group to praying for persecuted Christians. Read stories and take action through Voice of the Martyrs (*persecution.com*).

The increase of our joy in something produces a greater perseverance to obtain that joy more fully. This is why you see Peter and the apostles, after being beaten by the religious rulers, rejoicing:

> **"Then they went out from the presence of the Sanhedrin, rejoicing that they were counted worthy to be dishonored on behalf of the Name. Every day in the temple complex, and in various homes, they continued teaching and proclaiming the good news that Jesus is the Messiah" (Acts 5:41-42).**

It was their love of Jesus that compelled a beaten and whipped Paul and Silas to sing hymns in prison instead of drowning in a pool of self entitlement, valuing earthly or physical comfort over the Person and mission of Christ. It's worth pondering that professing followers of Jesus should be bothered more about *not* receiving rejection or reprisal than actually going through it.

What types of persecutions have you endured for your faith? How did you handle that persecution?*

Being prepared for Christ's return helps us face persecution and enables us to meet the needs of others who experience hardships. That makes our preparation very important.

In what ways does our faithfulness impact the world?

What can you do to ensure a continued faithfulness?

Revelation 7 provides a snapshot of what genuine obedience will do.

> **"After this I looked, and there was a vast multitude from every nation, tribe, people, and language, which no one could number, standing before the throne and before the Lamb. They were robed in white with palm branches in their hands" (v. 9).**

---

* Facilitator: What can you do to help your brothers and sisters who are suffering?

The apostle John saw evidence of the worldwide spread of the gospel in the innumerable people before the throne of God.

How should the knowledge of this scene affect the way we live now?

What do these passages imply about our faithfulness until Jesus returns?

My prayer for us is that we will be so motivated by Jesus' actions on our behalf, that no one and nothing will be able to deter us from sharing the love of God.

THIS WEEK REFLECT ON . . .

> CLOSING QUESTIONS
• What truth did you learn about Jesus this week? About the church?
• What does God desire for you personally and the church corporately to do in response to that truth?
• What steps can you take to guard your heart and keep it focused on God?
• How important is prayer and knowing the Word of God to you? What changes need to be made in your daily life?

> MAKING A CHANGE
• Read as many missionary biographies as you can get your hands on. Reading about the lives of missionaries, especially in non-Western areas of the world, has a way of knocking off our grip of self-reliance and compulsion toward comfort in this world.
• Ask God to reveal to you the people along your daily path who need to hear the gospel. Make an effort to foster spiritual conversations with them this week. If the door opens, share the gospel with them.

> GROWING WITH GOD
Pray, asking God to give you the same love for sharing the gospel that inspired the life of Philip. Read Romans 10:9-15 to conclude your prayer.

How do I defend the gospel?

by Derwin Gray

"Christians are now the foreigners in a post-Christian culture,
and we have got to wake up to this reality if we haven't."

—Dan Kimball,
They Like Jesus but Not the Church[1]

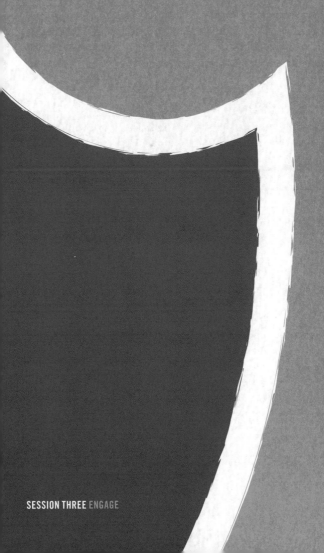

John met Ann in English 101. John was an atheist and Ann was raised in a Catholic family. Things were good until Ann met God at Transformation Church, where I have the honor of serving as founding and lead pastor. The more the gospel touched Ann's heart, the more Jesus transformed her life. As she fell in love with the God of great grace, she realized that her relationship with John had to end.

John couldn't understand why. Ann gently told John, "I love Jesus and you don't. Our lives are headed in different directions." She asked John if he would meet me, her pastor. John agreed.

Throughout this session, I'll walk you through some of the conversations I had with John. The goal is to identify some common questions nonbelievers have about the Bible and Christianity. We'll also explore how you can best answer these questions. Primarily we'll focus on the inner attitude of how to defend the gospel. From my conversation with John, I'll outline some basic questions and answers that will help you defend the gospel.*

ATHEIST MEETS THE PREACHER

The first thing I noticed about John when he walked into my office was how tall he was. Dude was about 6'6"! A former high school basketball player, John now was working toward a degree in broadcast journalism. His life goal was to be on ESPN as a sports anchor, and he already had started working for a local news station.

Just as when John and I talked, as we listen to someone's story, we connect with him or her at a heart level. Everyone has the need to connect. Let the wise words of the apostle Paul soak into your spiritual DNA:

LEARN TO LISTEN
Other than John's height, how did I know so much about him? Here is our first lesson in defending the gospel: Listen to people's stories, and as you do, you'll learn how to connect their story to God's.

"**Live wisely among those who are not believers, and make the most of every opportunity. Let your conversation be gracious and attractive so that you will have the right response for everyone**" (Colossians 4:5-6, NLT).

---

* Facilitator: How did you come to believe what you believe? What did the process of becoming a Christian look like for you?

Do you feel like you're a good listener? What are the benefits of listening to someone's story?

PEOPLE OF FAITH
Everyone, including an atheist, has faith in someone or something they hope will give them joy, an identity, and a purpose in life.*

EMOTIONAL, INTELLECTUAL, AND VOLITIONAL BARRIERS

John is a pleasant, intelligent twentysomething. He grew up in a home with both of his parents, who were also atheists. The first question John asked me is, "Atheism is all I've ever known; can you prove to me God exists and Jesus is that God?"

The simple answer? We can't "prove" God exists. If we could give 100 percent proof, we wouldn't need faith. What we can do is give some sign posts that God does exist and that Jesus is the Son of the God.

There are three barriers to people coming to faith: emotional, intellectual, and volitional. The Emotional Barrier occurs when someone has a bad experience with Christ-followers that leads to an emotional wound that never heals. The Intellectual Barrier occurs when people have questions that have not been answered concerning the faith. The Volitional Barrier occurs when Jesus requires the person to change his or her lifestyle to reflect God's values and they don't want to. Each of these barriers blinds them to the cross.

Which of these barriers have you struggled with in the past? How were you able to overcome it?

LIVE IN THE TENSION
As you share and defend the gospel, people may have one, or even all three, of these barriers blocking the beautiful, blood-soaked cross. Our privilege is to join the Holy Spirit in removing these barriers. Keep in mind, only the Spirit of God can lead someone to Jesus (John 6:44). But we can trust that the Spirit of God is working to draw all people to Jesus (John 12:32). Therefore, we can rest in the sacred tension of knowing that only God can draw people to God, yet how Christ-followers love each other plays a vital role in the world believing Jesus is the Savior (John 17:20-21).

---

* Facilitator: What do you think about the statement, "Everyone has faith in something that they hope will give them joy, an identity, and purpose in life"? How have you seen this played out in your circle of friends and family?

Read the following verses from John's Gospel:

> "No one can come to Me unless the Father who sent Me draws him, and I will raise him up on the last day" (John 6:44).

> "As for Me, if I am lifted up from the earth I will draw all people to Myself" (John 12:32).

> "I pray not only for these, but also for those who believe in Me through their message. May they all be one, as You, Father, are in Me and I am in You. May they also be one in Us, so the world may believe You sent Me" (John 17:20-21).

How do you explain the tension of partnering with God's Spirit in defending the gospel and trusting the Spirit to open hearts through our lives?

FOUR BASIC QUESTIONS

Atheists I've spoken with in the past have all seemed to struggle with four basic questions:

• Doesn't science prove that God doesn't exist?
• Why should I trust an outdated book like the Bible?
• How can God be loving, all-powerful, and good, with so much suffering and evil in the world?
• Is the resurrection of Jesus real?*

How do these questions compare with those you've been asked previously? Which one have you had the most trouble answering?

According to *livescience.com*, about two-thirds of scientists believe in God.

1. Doesn't science prove that God doesn't exist?
"From my understanding, it seems like science has proven that God doesn't exist."

John mistakenly thought all Christians were anti-science. Yet, it's important to understand that some atheistic scientists filter the scientific evidence through a philosophy called Naturalism. I believe there are three

---

* Facilitator: What other questions have you heard unbelievers express? How would you respond to their inquiries?

powerful sign posts from science that point to the existence of God. They are Big Bang cosmology, the fine-tuning of the universe, and biology.

Antony Flew, Ph.D., the world's leading atheist thinker for the last 50 years, has moved from atheism (There's no god.) to theism (There is a God.) because of these three sign posts from modern scientific observations:

> "I now believe that the universe was brought into existence by an infinite Intelligence. I believe that this universe's intricate laws manifest what scientists have called the Mind of God. I believe that life and reproduction originate in a divine source."[2]

How does science leave room for God?

After John and I talked, I had him read some books on modern scientific discoveries, so the next time we talked we could discuss what he learned.

Several months went by, John and I continued our conversation through email. Next time we met face-to-face, he said, "I can no longer honestly look at the scientific evidence and not believe there is a god, but I'm not sure this god is Jesus. I have some more questions for you about the Bible."

To learn more about Science Apologetics, here are some resources I recommend:
• The Creator and the Cosmos: How the Latest Scientific Discoveries of the Century Reveal God by Hugh Ross
• Origins of Life: Biblical and Evolutionary Models Face Off by Fazale Rana and Hugh Ross

PHILOSOPHICAL NATURALISM
"Philosophical naturalism is a worldview that claims that nature is a closed system of naturalistic causes and effects which cannot be influenced by anything from outside of nature; it follows that nature had to do the creating with no intervention from God. Dr. Scott C. Todd, a Kansas State University professor, accurately sums up naturalism; 'Even if all the data point to an intelligent designer, such a hypothesis is excluded from science because it is not naturalistic.' Do not miss the importance of his statement. Before the scientific data is even taken into account, philosophical naturalists have already decided that God cannot be involved in creation; this is philosophical naturalism, not science."
—Nancy Pearcy, *Total Truth*[3]

"Life at its root requires information, which is stored in DNA and protein molecules . . . The origin of information necessary to bring life into existence points toward God."
—Stephen C. Myer, *Where Science Meets Faith*

WALK WITH PEOPLE
In defending the gospel, walk with people. If you ask them to read a book, read it with them and discuss it. As you walk with people by reading the books you ask them to read, you discover that your faith will grow.

BIBLICAL RELIABILITY
To learn how to defend the historical reliability of Scripture, use the M-A-P-S method by Hank Hanegraaff to guide you: Manuscripts, Archaeology, Prophecy, Statistics (available online at *equip.org/PDF/DB011.pdf*).

- *The Case for a Creator: A Journalist Investigates Scientific Evidence That Points toward God* by Lee Strobel
- *There Is a God: How the World's Most Notorious Atheist Changed His Mind* by Antony Flew

2. Why should I trust an outdated book like the Bible?
First and foremost, the Bible is trustworthy because it's divine revelation, Holy Spirit inspired, and complete:

"For the word of the Lord is right, and all His work is trustworthy" (Psalm 33:4).

"Every word of God is pure" (Proverbs 30:5a).

"All Scripture is inspired by God and is profitable for teaching, for rebuking, for correcting, for training in righteousness, so that the man of God may be complete, equipped for every good work" (2 Timothy 3:16-17).

"No prophecy ever came by the will of man; instead, men spoke from God as they were moved by the Holy Spirit" (2 Peter 1:21).

Yet, for an unbeliever, we can't support the legitimacy of the Bible solely on its own word. We have to look at history, at the present day, and even within ourselves to see that God's Word is true and can be trusted.

What historical proof could you call upon to defend the truth of the Bible? Circle the items below that you need to further study.

- Jesus' empty tomb and post-resurrection appearances
- Roman historical accounts
- The Council of Nicaea
- Flavius Josephus, the first century historian
- The recorded prophesies of Jesus' birth, death, and resurrection
- The beginning and growth of the Christian church*
- Other:

---

* Facilitator: Take time to discuss each of these issues, according to the knowledge and needs of your group.

How can you validate the claims of Scripture based on the testimony of fellow Christians?

If you were called to speak on the impact God's Word and the Holy Spirit have had on your life, what would you say?

Even if someone believes that the Bible could be true, he or she can still struggle with individual issues—issues that keep him or her from faith in Jesus.

Have you ever walked into a movie, only to catch the last 30 minutes of it? It's impossible to accurately give a summary of that movie. This is often what happens when people cherry-pick a few hot button topics and draw a conclusion without understanding the entire plot of the story of God. Let's walk through a few of those hot-button issues:

Anti-Women
"Isn't the Bible against women?"

> **"So God created man in His own image; He created him in the image of God; He created them male and female"** (Genesis 1:27).

> **"There is no Jew or Greek, slave or free, male or female; for you are all one in Christ Jesus"** (Galatians 3:28).

The Bible is very clear: Men and women are equal. If anything, Jesus liberated women from being second-class citizens. The first person Jesus told that He was the Jewish Messiah was a woman (see John 4:4-42). And Jesus had women followers. Rabbis in the culture when Jesus lived would not even talk to their own wives or daughters in public, yet Jesus showed that women were equal with men by having women as His followers.

Women are a part of the priesthood of all believers, and as such, their time, talents, wisdom, and grace is crucial in fulfilling God's plan. And on a personal note, Transformation Church would not be the church she is today without the great females leaders we have.

In the development of the early church, women played a vital role in church leadership like Phoebe (Romans 16:1-2) and Priscilla (Acts 18:26; Romans 16:3-5). The apostle Paul's co-laborers were Euodia and Syntyche (Philippians 4:2-3).

What other biblical examples do we have of the important role of women in Christianity?

Homophobic

"The Bible is not progressing forward with culture concerning sexuality."

American culture isn't progressing forward sexually; it's actually digressing backward to the sexual ethics of ancient Rome. In ancient Rome, it was normative for a wealthy man to have little boys as their sex toys, orgies were a normative part of cultic temple worship practices, and gay and lesbian relationships were widely practiced.[4]

Emperor Nero himself lived a transgendered lifestyle.[5] He married a 12-year-old boy named Sporus, had him castrated, and dressed him as a woman. Then Nero married a man, Pythagora, who played the role of Nero's husband as Nero acted out the role of the wife.

I have several relatives in the Lesbian, Gay, Bisexual, and Transgender (LGBT) community. I love them and respect them. Every human being is made in the image of God, and therefore, they are worthy of respect and love. But that doesn't mean I have to agree with their sexual ethics. Nowhere in the Bible does it say our ethnicity or race is a sin, but it does say that certain behaviors are. Jesus Himself said,

To learn more on this most important issue, read chapter 8 in Dan Kimball's book, *They Like Jesus but Not The Church*, and chapter 5 in David Kinnaman's *Unchristian*. Both of these authors provide great insight.

"What comes out of a person is what defiles him. For from within, out of the heart of man, come evil thoughts, sexual immorality, theft, murder, adultery, coveting, wickedness, deceit, sensuality, envy, slander, pride, foolishness. All these evil things come from within, and they defile a person" (Mark 7:20-23, ESV).

The word for sexual immorality, *porneia*, means any sexual relationship outside of a heterosexual marriage; so any sex—gay or straight—outside of marriage is sin.

It's possible for a Christ-follower to say that homosexual activity is sinful, but people who have a homosexual orientation are to be loved and welcomed. There are people in my church who are attracted to people of the same sex, but by the Spirit's power, they choose not act on those feelings of attraction, just like I choose to not act on feelings for women other than my wife.

> "You are not to sleep with a man as with a woman; it is detestable" (Leviticus 18:22).

> "Therefore God delivered them over in the cravings of their hearts to sexual impurity, so that their bodies were degraded among themselves. They exchanged the truth of God for a lie, and worshiped and served something created instead of the Creator, who is praised forever" (Romans 1:24-25).

> "Don't you know that the unrighteous will not inherit God's kingdom? Do not be deceived: No sexually immoral people, idolaters, adulterers, or anyone practicing homosexuality, no thieves, greedy people, drunkards, verbally abusive people, or swindlers will inherit God's kingdom. And some of you used to be like this. But you were washed, you were sanctified, you were justified in the name of the Lord Jesus Christ and by the Spirit of our God" (1 Corinthians 6:9-11).

How do these passages of Scripture contribute to our understanding of homosexuality?

In your opinion, does the Bible prohibit the practice of homosexuality? Explain your answer.

Pro-Slavery
"How could you believe in a book that supports slavery?"

My religion professor had us read from Colossians:

> **"Slaves, obey your earthly masters in everything you do. Try to please them all the time, not just when they are watching you. Serve them sincerely because of your reverent fear of the Lord" (Colossians 3:22, NLT).**

In the first century Roman Empire, when the apostle Paul wrote this text, there wasn't much difference between a free person and a bondservant (slave). The bondservants earned money for their work, and they weren't segregated from society. Many of them eventually bought their freedom. Many became bondservants because they owed a debt and worked the debt off by serving the person they owed. Sadly, some Christians during the epic horror of American slavery used this verse to support the dehumanizing tragedy of American slavery. As Christians, we need to own that tragedy.

Additionally, the Bible records many sinful actions of man (murder, incest, rape, genocide, etc.). That doesn't mean Scripture condones these actions. Exodus explains how God went to great lengths to free His people from Pharoah's rule. Paul wrote in Philemon that Onesimus, a fugitive slave, should be treated not as a slave but as a brother in Christ (Philemon 1:8-22). Paul referred to himself as a willing "slave of Christ . . . singled out for God's good news" (Romans 1:1). Even God Himself sent His own Son as payment for our sins, to be freed from the oppression of sin (1 Corinthians 7:21-23).

How would you explain the difference between bondservants and slavery? between slavery of men and a slave of God?

---

* Facilitator: Have you updated your testimony recently? If not, take some time to write out suffering God has brought you through and blessings He has given you. Take time to rejoice in all He's done for you, and prayerfully consider who God might be leading you to share your testimony with.

3. How can God be loving, all-powerful, and good, with so much suffering and evil in the world?

I know a little about evil and suffering. I went through some very traumatic things as little boy and my wife has had cancer. I've stared death and evil in the face. The Christian faith doesn't expect the world to be free from evil, death, and suffering. We believe when Adam and Eve messed up in the garden of Eden, humanity and creation was broken— in need of a Savior.

Jesus said in this world we will have troubles but don't fear because He's overcome the world.

> **"I have told you these things so that in Me you may have peace. You will have suffering in this world. Be courageous! I have conquered the world" (John 16:33).**

> **"We know that all things work together for the good of those who love God: those who are called according to His purpose. For those He foreknew He also predestined to be conformed to the image of His Son, so that He would be the firstborn among many brothers" (Romans 8:28-29).**

> **"Consider it a great joy, my brothers, whenever you experience various trials, knowing that the testing of your faith produces endurance. But endurance must do its complete work, so that you may be mature and complete, lacking nothing" (James 1:2-4).**

SHARE YOUR TESTIMONY
No one can argue with your testimony. Share your story and how God has brought you through suffering and evil and how He has transformed you through that experience.

There are many reasons why God chooses to allow evil and suffering in this world (as a result of sin, for discipline, as part of His plan, as a way to bring us salvation through His Son, etc.). Every awful, painful thing that has ever happened to me, I now see how Jesus has worked through those difficult circumstances to transform me into the man I am.

SEEKING CERTAINTY
Are you uncertain when talking about your faith? Do you stumble over your words when someone asks you what you believe? Author Mary Jo Sharp, apologetics instructor and author of *Why Do You Believe That?*, discusses the importance of knowing what you believe, the fine art of sharing your faith, and why you should be prepared to defend your faith as a follower of Christ in an online video (available at *lifeway.com/article/video-mary-jo-sharp-knowing-sharing-defending-your-faith*).

How has God used pain and suffering to transform your life?

In the case of Jesus, how did God use pain and suffering as a positive thing for humanity?

4. Is the resurrection of Jesus real?

The evidence for the resurrection of Jesus is overwhelming. If all the evidence from Scripture, eyewitnesses, and history were lined up in a court room, there would be confirmation beyond all reasonable doubt that Christ had indeed risen.

Many of the New Testament books (Gospels and various epistles) were written soon after the reported events occurred. Time simply didn't allow for legends and myths to enter into the biblical accounts.[*]

The gospel writers also gave careful attention to details. They related specific facts of Jesus' historical time period (including names, dates, events, customs, etc.). Historically speaking, the central criterion for including the Gospels in the New Testament canon was that they emerged from eyewitnesses or associates of eyewitnesses.

EVIDENCE OF THE RESURRECTION

• Jesus' brutal torture and death
• The empty tomb
• His post-resurrection appearances
• The transformation of followers from cowards to missionaries and martyrs

Since good evidence supports the conclusion that the Gospels (the Books of Matthew, Mark, Luke, and John) are early sources, one can reasonably argue that if the gospel writers had departed from the historical facts (either by exaggeration or outright invention), hostile witnesses familiar with the events of Jesus' life could have and would have exposed them.

---

* Facilitator: Take time to discuss common myths and legends and what evidence we have against those misconceptions.

Viewing the resurrection of Jesus Christ as a legend or myth ignores the solid historical support behind the event, seems deeply rooted in unsupported antisupernatural presuppositions, and fails to reflect the short interval of time between the emergence of the Gospels themselves and the actual events reported and described.

So why do people still struggle to believe?

Accepting the resurrection isn't just an issue of evidence but also an issue of faith. Only when we recognize our sinful nature and trust that God alone offers forgiveness and a chance at a new kind of life do we fully grasp the significance of the resurrection. Then the reality of the resurrection comes into focus. Christ's death atoned for our sinfulness and an empty tomb stands as evidence.

The resurrection of Jesus, is a foretaste of what will happen to creation and every person who believes that He is the resurrection and life.

RECOMMENDED READING LIST

General Apologetics

- *The Reason for God* by Tim Keller
- *That's Just Your Interpretation* by Paul Copan
- *Is God Just a Human Invention? And Seventeen Other Questions Raised by the New Atheists* by Sean McDowell and Jonathan Morrow
- *Is the Bible Intolerant? Sexist? Oppressive? Homophobic? Outdated? Irrelevant?* by Amy Orr-Ewing
- *The Case for Christ* and *The Case for Faith* by Lee Strobel
- *I Don't Have Enough Faith to Be an Atheist* by Norm Geisler and Frank Turek
- *They Like Jesus but Not the Church* by Dan Kimball
- *Apologetics for a New Generation* by Sean McDowell (general editor)

Incarnational Apologetics

- *Limitless Life: You Are More Than Your Past When God Holds Your Future* by Derwin L. Gray

God's world is broken because of human sin. But God the Father moved by love for His creation sent His Son Jesus to suffer every ounce of pain and injustice the world has known or will ever know. On the cross, Jesus suffered and defeated sin, death, and evil through His resurrection. The Church grew as a result of Jesus' death and resurrection, and it is Jesus' body, the visible expression His life.

> "He demonstrated this power in the Messiah by raising Him from the dead and seating Him at His right hand in the heavens—far above every ruler and authority, power and dominion, and every title given, not only in this age but also

in the one to come. And He put everything under His feet and appointed Him as head over everything for the church, which is His body, the fullness of the One who fills all things in every way" (Ephesians 1:20-23).

Salvation isn't about escaping planet earth; it's Eternal Life Himself, Jesus, forging a community of people who become the means of grace that restore our broken world.

"Then I saw a new heaven and a new earth, for the first heaven and the first earth had passed away, and the sea no longer existed. I also saw the Holy City, new Jerusalem, coming down out of heaven from God, prepared like a bride adorned for her husband. Then I heard a loud voice from the throne: Look! God's dwelling is with humanity, and He will live with them. They will be His people, and God Himself will be with them and be their God. He will wipe away every tear from their eyes. Death will no longer exist; grief, crying, and pain will exist no longer, because the previous things have passed away" (Revelation 21:1-4).

What alternative explanation do you offer to the New Testament documentation and the tradition of the church, and what support do you have for your theory?

Several months went by and I didn't hear from John. One afternoon, I noticed in my inbox an email from John. He said, "I was up one night praying and something I can't explain happened. I will be in Charlotte soon. Can we meet again?"

The next time I saw John he hugged me and said, "I get it. I believe Jesus is the Son of God. He is my Savior." I said, "John, what happened?" He said,

"The more I read the Bible, the books you wanted me to read, and the more I listened to your sermons[6] and prayed, something happened that I can't explain other than I just believed."

John and Ann are now engaged.

THIS WEEK REFLECT ON . . .

> CLOSING QUESTIONS
• What is God saying to you as a result of working through this session?
• What questions that non-Christians might have are you still struggling to answer? Take time this week to do more research in preparation for sharing your faith with others.

> GROWING WITH GOD
In his devotional classic, *Abide in Christ,* Andrew Murray wrote: "As the believer enters into his calling as a branch, he sees that he has to forget himself, and to live entirely for his fellowmen. To love them, to seek for them, and to save them. Jesus came: for this every branch on the Vine has to live as much as the Vine itself. It is for fruit, much fruit, that the Father had made us one with Jesus."[7]

One of the best ways to help prepare yourself for adversity in sharing your faith is by investing in your relationship with Jesus. Christians are called to glorify Him, yield to Him, and love and serve others in His name. Strengthening this relationship has a direct effect on the quality of your witness to others. When you submit and lean into God—abide in Him— He enables you to bear fruit.

> MAKING A CHANGE
Most people are ready and willing to express their opinions on any given subject. True listeners and genuine observers, however, are much harder to find. Next time you want to share Christ with someone, tell them about something you recently experienced that was meaningful to you. You just might be surprised at the conversation that follows.

> FOR FURTHER STUDY
Choose one of the studies listed in this session to continue seeking ways to defend your faith.

How do I share the gospel?

by Ben Reed

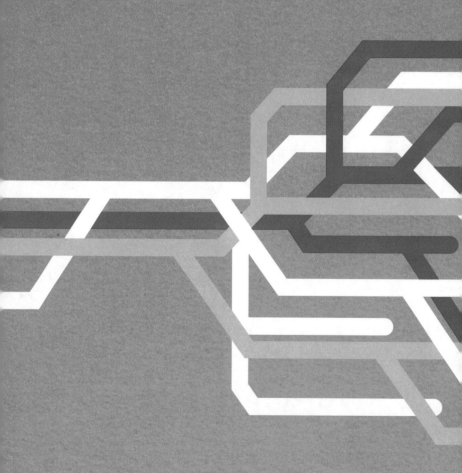

"I've seen far too many Christians who are more than willing to travel halfway around the world to volunteer for a week in an orphanage, but who cannot bring themselves to take the personal risk of sharing Jesus with the hell-bound co-worker who sits day after day in the cubicle right next to them."
—Lee Strobel, "Shortchanging the Good News"[1]

If you're anything like me, witnessing comes super-easily. It seems I can winsomely turn every conversation I have back to the foundations of the gospel, have people laughing, nodding their head in agreement, crying, and saying, "Amen!" within just a few minutes. I quote a verse, and people cry out, "Please, more truth, Ben!" I sing a hymn while walking down the sidewalk, and people never look at me like I'm a freak . . . Nay, they begin singing along, raising their hands in worship. I just have to encourage them not to close their eyes while they're walking!

I carry tracts in my pocket, because every time I meet an unbeliever and give them one, they ask me if I'll baptize them on the spot. I say, "It seems you need to hear about Jesus . . ." and they immediately respond, saying, "Yes, I've been waiting all my life! Please tell me more . . ." I always have the perfect word to say, the perfect prayer to pray, the perfect timing, and the perfect closing.

Don't you?

No?!? Yeah, me neither. To me, witnessing is tough. It often feels stilted, forced, and unnatural. I never seem to have the right timing. And trying to perfectly remember each point about the gospel, combined with the fact that I'm nervous—that I feel like the other person hates me for bringing it up, that I feel woefully inadequate to share, that I feel like I have no idea what I'm talking about, that I just know that the other person has to be somewhere else and do something else—makes sharing my faith one of the most difficult activities I ever do.

What's the most difficult part of starting a conversation about the gospel for you?

RETHINKING OUR APPROACH
I think we make sharing the gospel too difficult, though. I know I do. When it comes to evangelism, let me offer you three steps to think through.

1. Follow
Follow Christ. That's what He calls each of us to do, right? You, living the

life God has called you to live and being the person God has uniquely gifted you to be—that's a great testimony to God. Each of us are a walking billboard for the goodness of God and a testimony that God can redeem, right, and set straight a person's life. You don't have to be perfect. Nobody expects you to be flawless. (Gasp!) And if you try to portray that to people, you'll come across as arrogant, hypocritical, and fake. You don't have to have a perfect testimony, but you do have to follow a perfect Savior. That's essential.

2. Share

Share your story. Your story is compelling. Riveting. Life-changing (assuming you actually have been changed). And sharing your faith involves sharing your story. Be honest, transparent, and vulnerable. People will connect with your brokenness more quickly and fully than they ever will your "awesomeness." Share the mistakes God's redeeming you from, the sin you're done with, the bigger picture He's inviting you into, and the ways His grace is sufficient and His love is captivating.*

CHRISTIANITY: DOING VS. BEING

Being a Christian and sharing God's Word, at its core, means loving and caring for the people Christ puts in your world.

We're surrounded by people everyday—the people we work with, those we live next door to, and those who ride the train or bus with us. Everywhere we look, we will see people, those hurting and needing to experience God's love and mercy.

Don't give them a tract or a canned gospel presentation—although those things do have their place—and think you've done your evangelistic duty. Love on them. Leave a bigger tip in Jesus' name. Have a dinner party in Jesus' name. Mow your neighbor's yard in Jesus' name. Pray for more opportunities in Jesus' name.

Right now, where you are, begin rethinking evangelism. Begin to see it as much more than something you do and more of something you are.

3. Invite

Invite other people into your story. Build relationships with people. And not just so that you can "get them saved." Genuinely love people. Invest in them. Be their friend. Listen to their stories. Value them as God's crowning creation. Look for ways to serve them, expecting nothing in return and with no strings attached. In so doing, you're inviting them into the story that God's writing through you. I'm convinced that people want to plug into something that's bigger than themselves. Inviting people into your story, showing how your story fits into the broader story of God's redemption of His people, does just that.

---

* Facilitator: In what ways have you believed the lie that your story of faith isn't compelling? How has that stopped you from telling it in the past?

How can you make yourself more available for God to use in sharing Christ with those in your sphere of influence?*

THAT'S ALL?

That's it. Sharing your faith is much less complicated than we (church leaders) often make it. But it's also much more difficult. Much more engaging. Much more demanding of your time and effort. Much more challenging of your life.

Believing in Jesus and all He's done for us should . . .

- drive us to love others more, not less.
- move us toward people, not away from them.
- move us to condemn less, and love more.
- propel us toward kindness and patience, breaking our hearts for those far from Christ.
- drive us to serve others, looking for nothing in return.

"Millions of people, both inside and outside the church, believe that the essential message of Christianity is, 'If you behave, then you belong.' From a human standpoint, that's why most people reject Christianity. A friend of mine told me the other day that the reason his now-deceased father never went to church was that he didn't think he was good enough. He said his dad thought church was all about a good person telling other good people how to be better people. But that's not what the Bible says."

—Tullian Tchividjian, *Jesus + Nothing = Everything*[2]

"All day long I have spread out My hands to a disobedient and defiant people" (Romans 10:21).

What does it mean to you that every person is "disobedient and defiant" toward God?

How should that change the way you approach non-Christians? How does it affect the way you approach God?

All. Day. Long. God's hands are full of hope, love, mercy, grace, forgiveness, and blessing. He sent His Son to earth to have a relationship with us. Let's not reduce the beauty and power of that to mere words. To do so rips the truth of its love, grace, and mercy.

---

* Facilitator: Brainstorm three lists with your group: 1. Normal places you go where opportunities my arise to share the gospel. 2. Reasons why we should love to tell others about Jesus. 3. Foundational truths of the gospel that should be included when we do share.

Follow Christ. Share your story. Invite people in. It's that simple.

Without love, truth is … Obnoxious. Offensive. Impersonal. Insignificant.

What evidence supports this statement?

Write your faith story out. Right now. The three-minute version, with no "churchy" words.

What do you notice about your story? In what parts of your story can others find themselves?

IS HAVING A PLAN WRONG?

Am I saying we should only engage people organically, never having thought through how we'd actually walk someone from "death to life" (John 5:24)? Am I implying that if we have a step-by-step plan, we're not trusting the Spirit? That the ABCs of salvation is dangerous?

Not at all.

_____

5 TIPS FOR SHARING THE GOSPEL

• You don't work on commission. Too often bridges are burned and people are offended when you push them to decisions they're not ready to make. As urgent as the gospel message may be, try hard not to come off like a salesman. Be OK with, "Let me think about that."

• Talk about similarities. Yes, there are differences between Christians and non-Christians, but don't feel like you must point them all out. Remember that you're both human, selfish sinners. It's good to talk about what you once were, but be careful not to paint the wrong picture of "Now I am better than you."

• Analogies are great; direct truth is better. Sometimes telling stories and analogies can really help demonstrate the truth of Christ, but don't focus on a great analogy. Focus on a great Savior.

• Eat something. Food helps to pace conversation and provides a reason to get together. Stick to fast and casual. Waiting on food and an answer to an important question can be very uncomfortable.

• Develop your relationship. Nothing says "I love you" more than taking time to get to know someone. They're not your "project"; they're lost people who need to see the love of Christ modeled through your life.

I'm just saying you shouldn't depend on those tools solely. Evangelism tools are incredibly helpful in the context of a relationship, couched with the depth and beauty of your story and how it links with how God is working in others' lives.

For my bachelor party before I got married, my buddies threw me a tool party. It was awesome. I got all kinds of great tools: a hammer, a driver set, screwdrivers, and . . . an amp measuring tool. "I love mine," he said as I opened it. "Wow. Thanks!" I said, as I began wondering what in the world I was supposed to do with it.

In the hands of a skilled worker, that tool was indispensable. It would help them accomplish great projects, making life easier and more efficient for them. In the hands of someone who is, admittedly, not great with projects that involve electricity, it's dangerous. It could hurt me and others. Even though I had the best intentions and the right projects, I could never use it to its full potential.

Though tools are helpful, they've got to be used in their right context by people who know what they're doing.

Evangelism tools like the ones we're going to discuss are best shared in the context of a relationship—not blindly with random passersby. Can shout outs of truth at the mall work to lead someone to a saving knowledge of faith? Sure. But that's not how they're used most effectively.[*]

---

[*] Facilitator: Share your own story with the large group. Then pair into groups to give each person practice sharing their own unique stories in front of others.

Think through the different evangelism methods you've been exposed to. Which, if any, of the methods did you find to be effective? What about the experiences made you uncomfortable?

"One thing I have observed in all my years of ministry is that the most effective and important aspects of evangelism usually take place on an individual, personal level. Most people do not come to Christ as an immediate response to a sermon they hear in a crowded setting. They come to Christ because of the influence of an individual."

—John MacArthur, *Twelve Ordinary Men*

TOOLS OF THE TRADE

Let's look at a few different models. Memorize the one you think is most helpful. Or the one that you feel like connects most easily with your story. Or, heck, just memorize one because that's the first one you came to. It doesn't so much matter what your plan is. Just have a plan that will focus and guide you to action.

Utilize these tools as you're building a relationship with someone, sharing your story, giving them a chance to express their brokenness, and weeping or laughing with them.

1. William Fay's questions to turn a conversation to spiritual things:
• Do you have any kind of spiritual belief?
• To you, who is Jesus?
• Do you think there is a heaven or a hell?
• If you died right now, where would you go?
• If what you believe were not true, would you want to know it?[3]

2. As Easy as A.B.C.
A — *Admit* that you're a sinner, and that no good that you can do earns you God's love and forgiveness (Romans 3:23; 6:23; see also Acts 3:19; 1 John 1:9).

B — *Believe* that Jesus is God's Son and that God sent His Son to save us from our sins. This belief should always motivate love (John 3:16; 14:6; Romans 5:8).

C — *Confess* your faith in Christ (Romans 10:9-10,13).

3. All Roads Lead To . . .

The Roman Road

Romans 3:23 — "For all have sinned and fall short of the glory of God."

Romans 6:23 — "For the wages of sin is death, but the gift of God is eternal life in Christ Jesus our Lord."

Romans 5:8 — "But God proves His own love for us in that while we were still sinners, Christ died for us!"

Romans 10:9-10 — "If you confess with your mouth, 'Jesus is Lord,' and believe in your heart that God raised Him from the dead, you will be saved. One believes with the heart, resulting in righteousness, and one confesses with the mouth, resulting in salvation."

The John Road

John 3:16 — "For God loved the world in this way: He gave His One and Only Son, so that everyone who believes in Him will not perish but have eternal life."

John 6:44 — "No one can come to Me unless the Father who sent Me draws him, and I will raise him up on the last day."

John 14:6 — "Jesus told him, 'I am the way, the truth, and the life. No one comes to the Father except through Me.'"

John 1:12 — "But to all who did receive Him, He gave them the right to be children of God, to those who believe in His name."

The 1 John Road

1 John 1:8-9 — "If we say, 'We have no sin,' we are deceiving ourselves, and the truth is not in us. If we confess our sins, He is faithful and righteous to forgive us our sins and to cleanse us from all unrighteousness."

1 John 3:16 — "This is how we have come to know love: He laid down His life for us. We should also lay down our lives for our brothers."

1 John 4:15 — "Whoever confesses that Jesus is the Son of God—God remains in him and he in God."

1 John 5:13 — "I have written these things to you who believe in the name of the Son of God, so that you may know that you have eternal life."

The Ephesians Road
Ephesians 2:1-10 is about the clearest presentation of the full gospel as you can find in any one passage of Scripture.

> "And you were dead in your trespasses and sins in which you previously walked according to the ways of this world, according to the ruler who exercises authority over the lower heavens, the spirit now working in the disobedient. We too all previously lived among them in our fleshly desires, carrying out the inclinations of our flesh and thoughts, and we were by nature children under wrath as the others were also. But God, who is rich in mercy, because of His great love that He had for us, made us alive with the Messiah even though we were dead in trespasses. You are saved by grace! Together with Christ Jesus He also raised us up and seated us in the heavens, so that in the coming ages He might display the immeasurable riches of His grace through His kindness to us in Christ Jesus. For you are saved by grace through faith, and this is not from yourselves; it is God's gift—not from works, so that no one can boast. For we are His creation, created in Christ Jesus for good works, which God prepared ahead of time so that we should walk in them."

Meditate on this. Get it in your heart and in your mind. Chew on the parts that resonate with you the most. Then you'll always have the Scripture that reminds you of the truth and hope of the gospel.

What role has Scripture study and memorization played in your walk with Christ so far? How can that shape your future witness for Him?

---

4. You Gotta Have F.A.I.T.H.

In your personal opinion, what do you understand it takes for a person to go to heaven? Consider how the Bible answers this question. It's a matter of FAITH.

F is for *Forgiveness*. We cannot have eternal life and heaven without God's forgiveness.

> **"We have redemption in Him through His blood, the forgiveness of our trespasses" (Ephesians 1:7a).**

A is for *Available*. Forgiveness is available for all.

> **"For God loved the world in this way: He gave His One and Only Son, so that everyone who believes in Him will not perish but have eternal life" (John 3:16).**

But it's not automatic.

> **"Not everyone who says to Me, 'Lord, Lord!' will enter the kingdom of heaven" (Matthew 7:21a).**

I is for *Impossible*. It is impossible for God to allow sin into heaven.

Because of who He is: God is loving and just. His judgment is against sin.

> **"For judgment is without mercy to the one who hasn't shown mercy" (James 2:13a).**

Because of who we are: Every person is a sinner.

> **"For all have sinned and fall short of the glory of God" (Romans 3:23).**

But how can a sinful person enter heaven, when God allows no sin?

T is for *Turn*. Turn means repent from sin and self.

> **"Unless you repent, you will all perish as well" (Luke 13:3b).**

Turn to Someone; trust Christ only.

> **"If you confess with your mouth, 'Jesus is Lord,' and believe in your heart that God raised Him from the dead, you will be saved" (Romans 10:9).**

H is for *Heaven*. Heaven is eternal life.

> **"I have come so that they may have life and have it in abundance" (John 10:10b).**

> **"If I go away and prepare a place for you, I will come back and receive you to Myself, so that where I am you may be also" (John 14:3).**

How? How can a person have God's forgiveness, heaven, and eternal life, and Jesus as personal Savior and Lord? By trusting in Christ and asking Him for forgiveness.*

5. Party with the Sinners

The last example I'll give is all about your lifestyle. How do you approach unbelievers? Are you willing to spend time with them and be bold enough to keep a strong witness?

Right after Levi became a follower of Jesus (see Mark 2:14), what do you think he did?

a. Became a church member
b. Started tithing
c. Committed to reading through the Bible in a year
d. Threw a party

If you guessed "d," you're right! Check this out:

> **"While He was reclining at the table in Levi's house, many tax collectors and sinners were also guests with Jesus and His disciples, because there were many who were following Him" (Mark 2:15).**

---

* **Facilitator:** If it seems appropriate, take turns discussing what forgiveness has meant to you and the role that plays in your willingness to share your faith with others.

You know why there were tax collectors here at this party? Because that's who Levi was. He had been a tax collector. So Levi walked away from his job, but he didn't walk away from his relationships. He walked away from his job because his job was sinful. But these relationships were different now. He was introducing them to Jesus.

Levi didn't run away from relationships with those outside of the church. He ran toward them, inviting them into his home for a meal. Which would've been expensive, right? Ever tried to feed a lot of people in your home? It's expensive and messy, but it's worth your time and effort.

These people aren't Christ followers yet. They're far from Christ. They're tax collectors! They're people who wouldn't step a foot in a church building.

You know people like this. Invite them into your home to build relationships and introduce them to Jesus.

Be in the habit of inviting your friends, neighbors, co-workers, and so forth into your home to serve them.

We've walked through five different tools. Which did you connect with most? Why?*

In a safe environment, share these tools with someone and ask for feedback. Think about this as a practice for the big game.

Who could you invite, who doesn't know Jesus, to your home for a meal? Write their names below:

_____

* Facilitator: For those experiencing fear and uncertainty in sharing their faith, spend time studying the story of Ananias and Saul in Acts 9. Discuss how Ananias' yes to God to witness to Saul changed the course of the Christian church forever.

How would you show them the love of Jesus without simply putting a tract in their hands?

A GLOBAL CALLING

Take a moment to think outside of your circle of family and friends. God doesn't call us to minister and witness to only those in our communities; He calls us to go across the globe:

> **"You will be My witnesses in Jerusalem, in all Judea and Samaria, and to the ends of the earth"** (Acts 1:8b).

"Preach abroad. It is the cooping yourselves up in rooms that has dampened the work of God, which never was and never will be carried out to any purpose without going into the highways and hedges and compelling men and women to come in."
—Jonathan Edwards

Global missions can seem a little strange when faced with all the needs in our own community. Whether it be in disaster relief, unchurched Native American tribes, or even helping out the elderly next door, there's plenty of God's work to do within our country.

But the need to go into the entire world with the gospel of Christ is huge, and there's great benefit for global missions beyond the meeting of physical needs. Here's an interesting look at the value of global missions:

- Going to a foreign culture helps create a broader view of the kingdom of God both for the missionary and those being served.

- The fact that someone would travel halfway around the world to share about Christ heightens the importance of the message for the hearer.

- Seeing the pairing of extreme poverty and Christianity is something that will forever change the life of a Christian who has an abundance back home.

For more ideas on how to share the gospel, download the "THE ACT Principle: How to Start a Conversation about Spiritual Things" worksheet (available online at *threadsmedia. com/downloads/ beachreach_the_act_ principle.pdf*).

---

* Facilitator: Be prepared to share what tool you've successfully used in the past.

PLACES TO TELL OTHERS ABOUT CHRIST

1. AT THE GROCERY STORE. No one expects you to stand outside the store and preach, but while you're picking up your weekly groceries, offer a friendly smile at those around you. While standing in line, strike up a conversation with the person in front of you. Ask how you can pray for them this week.

2. AT THE COFFEE SHOP. You're in the drive-thru line for your regular latte. If you have the money and time, pay for the person behind you. Ask the cashier to write a Bible verse of your choice on the cup. You won't only minister to the person behind you but to the cashier as well. A two-for-one-deal.

3. AT WORK. You don't have to say much, but every now and then you can mention how God is working in your life. Your coworkers may be unresponsive at first, but pray for them regularly, and see if they open up to you.

4. IN CLASS. If you're in college, before the big chemistry exam, ask the classmates sitting closest to you if they'd like to pray with you for good grades. It may be a simple prayer, but it might help offer your classmates peace of mind during the test.

5. IN LINE. Any time you're in a line, be kind to those around you. Usually a friendly conversation can help a person be more apt to listen. And when you're all stuck in a long line, you have an easy way to share the love of Christ with them.

• Human effort is weakened in other countries because of language differences, cultural misunderstandings, and a lack of supplies. Our human weakness brings with it God's strength.

What other reasons can you give why both domestic and foreign missions are important?

Have you ever moved outside your own cultural comfort zone for the sake of helping someone different from you understand the gospel? What was the result?*

Which of the following am I willing to risk to share the gospel: job security, family affection, friendships or other relationships, reputation, life? Pray specifically for the boldness to be willing to risk all of the above for the spread of the gospel.

THE NEXT STEPS

So you've built the relationships. You've shown others by the way you live and the way you love that you follow a King full of grace and mercy. In fact, you even took it a step further, and shared your faith in a tangible way with a tool that you found helpful. And they responded!

***Facilitator:** Discuss how your group can work together to bless others. Those blessings can be money, but just as important is the outpouring of conversation, time, prayer, energy, and materials.

A Positive Response

You've shared the gospel with your friend and he or she wants to start a new life with Christ. What do you do? Don't panic! This is reason for celebration!

Here are a few simple actions to help affirm someone in his or her new walk with Christ:

1. Pray with them. Encourage them to repeat a prayer after you that covers three things:

   a. confession that they need forgiveness from God
   b. recognition that Jesus' death in our place is the only hope we have for forgiveness
   c. commitment to live in a way that honors God and seeks to live a new life for Him

2. Share an encouraging verse with them that emphasizes the significance of the moment. Make it personal by sharing a favorite verse of yours, or here are a couple that would work great: John 10:29; Romans 8:38-39; and Ephesians 2:8-10.

3. Set up a time to meet again to talk about next steps of discipleship. In the meantime, think through the other follow-up suggestions (below) and come prepared to talk through them with your friend

But what now? Are you done? Is your work complete? You've done what you needed to do, and now you can move on?

Not so fast.

The Great Commission doesn't compel us to just "convert" someone. We're called to make disciples. Our responsibility doesn't end when they say "yes." God has called us to much more!

The pathway to growing in faith involves a few "next steps."

1. Baptism. Christian baptism is the immersion of a believer in water in the name of the Father, the Son, and the Holy Spirit. It's an act of obedience symbolizing the believer's faith in a crucified, buried, and risen Savior and

the believer's death to sin, the burial of the old life, and the resurrection to walk in the new life her or she has in Christ. And it's a great chance to preach the gospel to people who are watching!

2. Regular worship. Invite them to join you on Sunday morning in worship. Regular worship feeds our soul as we connect with God corporately. It's vital to our faith.

3. Small group. Without other people in our lives who love us, care for us, and want God's best for us, our faith will shrivel up. What was once a burning passion will be a lump of dry coals. And this process takes much less time than you'd think. Introduce them to a small group. Or, better yet, just start a small group of your own with them!

Each of these steps helps new believers understand that their relationship with Christ goes much deeper than a one-time decision. God wants to redeem every aspect of their lives. And these few things—following Jesus in baptism, regular worship, and journeying through life with others—are great steps to take right out of the gate.

Relationships are key to leading someone to a saving faith in Christ, and they're key to someone's continued growth in faith. So quickly introduce him to others who can speak into his life. If she is going to grow in her faith, she'll need more than your voice continuing to point her to Jesus. Help her connect with others in meaningful ways.

What "next step" should you help them take? What's an easy way for them to take a step of faith?

If someone said "yes" to you right now, who could you introduce that person to that's a little further down the road of faith? Write down three names below.

_____

What verses in the Bible could you point someone to who had just accepted Jesus as his or her Savior? How could you help disciple that person?

A Negative Response

So you had a conversation about your faith with someone and he didn't respond like you'd hoped. She shrugged you off and turned the other way.* Or he responded positively in the moment, but now, two weeks later, he's right back in his same old habits before saying "yes" to Jesus.

Since you've built a relationship with them, though, your chances to share hope aren't over. The truth you shared wasn't in a vacuum but built around love. They may have said, "No" to your message, but they haven't said, "No" to you as a person. So you keep loving them and continue the conversation.

When others respond negatively:

1. Keep trusting God. And at the end of the day, it's God who saves, not you. All you can do is be faithful with what God puts in front of you, and trust that God is working even when what you're doing doesn't seem to be.

> **"What then is Apollos? And what is Paul? They are servants through whom you believed, and each has the role the Lord has given. I planted, Apollos watered, but God gave the growth. So then neither the one who plants nor the one who waters is anything, but only God who gives the growth"** (1 Corinthians 3:5-7).

2. Keep praying for them. You believe prayer works, right? Then why stop now! Continue your conversation with God about them. Don't give up pleading with Him. God's timing isn't our timing. His wisdom isn't our wisdom. And His power isn't our power.

3. Keep giving grace. You don't know what part of their story you're playing. You don't know how your faithfulness will pay dividends in their

---

* Facilitator: Discuss appropriate immediate responses when a person tells you "no" after sharing your faith.

life spiritually. You don't know where they'll go next, who they'll meet, how their life will change, and where their next steps will take them. Keep your posture one of grace and love.

Whatever you do, don't give up on your relationship with them. Don't stop loving them. Don't stop offering grace. Don't walk away from the foundation you've built. The Truth is bigger than a series of propositional facts. Live and love the gospel actively, as you have been doing already.

Have you recently gotten a "no" from someone? What did you do after that rejection?

Did your relationship change with the "no"?

What have you done (or what could you do) to continue to show grace and love to this person?

Whatever your plan is, whoever the people are that God brings across your path, may your cry always be,

> "As for us, there's no question—we can't keep quiet about what we've seen and heard" (Acts 4:20, MSG).

THIS WEEK REFLECT ON . . .

> CLOSING QUESTIONS
- What gifts has God given you that could be used to minister to others in a mission endeavor? Where might He be calling you to use those gifts?
- What are some things you could look or listen for that might help you to know how to begin to be a witness for Christ?
- In addition to verbal witness, how can we share the gospel in places we go? In what sense do we represent Christ in all those places?

> GROWING WITH GOD
One of the most important aspects of sharing is seeking God's will through prayer. God's will might not remove us from difficult situations or soften our trek through life by delivering us from opposition, but when we pray God will strengthen us and make us more effective for Him in those situations. God furnishes boldness and courage to His people when they need it. Honest prayer releases God's power and invites God's hand to work through our communities. Look for it. Seize it. Know that it goes before you as you boldly serve and share about Him.

> MAKING A CHANGE
- If you haven't already, write out your testimony of salvation, focusing on when you met Jesus and the transformation He brought to your life.
- Practice sharing your testimony with a good friend or family member this week so that it becomes comfortable to talk about.
- Go ask someone their faith story. Try listening without thinking about what you're going to say next.
- Repeat the last one until someone asks you what your faith story is.

END NOTES

SESSION 1

1. J.D. Greear, *Gospel: Recovering the Power that Made Christianity Revolutionary* (Nashville, TN: B&H, 2011), 5.
2. Adapted from J.D. Greear's books, *Gospel: Recovering the Power that Made Christianity Revolutionary* and *Stop Asking Jesus Into Your Heart: How To Know For Sure You Are Saved.*
3. Tim Keller, *Center Church* (Grand Rapids, MI: Zondervan, 2012), 29.
4. "On Passive Righteousness," a paraphrase and abridgment from Martin Luther's preface to his commentary on Galatians (November 4, 2012). Available online at *www.livingwatercc.org.*
5. "Teleo," HCSB Study Bible (Nashville, TN: Holman Bible Publishers, 2010), 1848.
6. C. S. Lewis, *Mere Christianity* (New York: HarperCollins, 1952), 56.
7. Dave Hunt, "God So Loved . . . !" The Berean Call, December 1, 2004. Available from *www.thebereancall.org.*
8. Adapted from Laura Magness, "Jesus Lives in Us," LifeMatters blog. Available at *www.threadsmedia.com.*

SESSION 2

1. Martin Luther, *Preface to the New Testament, 1522,* as quoted in *Martin Luther: Selections from His Writings, John Dillenbergen,* ed (New York: Anchor Books, 1962), 18.
2. C. S. Lewis, *Reflections on the Psalms* (Boston: Houghton Mifflin Harcourt, 1964), 95.
3. Adapted from *The Art of Personal Evangelism: Sharing Christ in a Changing Culture* by Will McRaney Jr. (Broadman & Holman Publishers, 2003).
4. Tim Keller, "The Centrality of the Gospel," Redeemercitytocity.com. Available online at *http://redeemercitytocity.com.*
5. Matt Tullos, adapted from "Six Ways to Choose Wonder," *Collegiate* Summer 2012. Used by permission.
6. Jerry Bridges, available online at *www.modernreformation.org.*

SESSION 3

1. Dan Kimball, *They Like Jesus but Not the Church: Insights from Emerging Generations* (Grand Rapids, MI: Zondervan, 2007), 30.
2. Antony Flew, *There Is A God: How the World's Most Notorious Atheist Changed His Mind* (New York: Harper One, 2007), 88.
3. Nancy Pearcy, *Total Truth* (Wheaton, IL: Tyndale, 1999); Scott C. Todd, Biology Department, Kansas State University, 168.

4. Amy Orr-Ewing, *Is the Bible Intolerant? Sexist? Oppressive? Homophobic? Outdated? Irrelevant?* (Downers Grove, IL: IVP Books, 2005), 114.
5. "The letters to the Corinthians," 1975 (W. Barclay, Ed.). *The Daily Study Bible Series* (53–54). Philadelphia, PA: The Westminster John Knox Press.
6. For further study, Derwin Gray's sermons from Transformation Church are available online at *transformationchurch.tc/sermons/archive.php.*
7. Andrew Murray, *Abide in Christ* (New Kensington, PA: Whitaker House, 1979), 38.

SESSION 4
1. Lee Strobel, "Shortchanging the Good News," ChurchLeaders.com. Accessed May 24, 2013. Available at *www.churchleaders.com.*
2. Tullian Tchividjian, *Jesus + Nothing = Everything* (Wheaton, IL: Crossway, 2011), 53.
3. Adapted from William Fay and Ralph Hodge, *Share Jesus Without Fear,* revised edition (Nashville, TN: LifeWay Press, 2008).

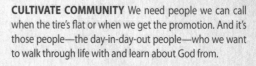

Threads

An advocate of churches and people like you, Threads provides Bible studies and events designed to:

CULTIVATE COMMUNITY We need people we can call when the tire's flat or when we get the promotion. And it's those people—the day-in-day-out people—who we want to walk through life with and learn about God from.

PROVIDE DEPTH Kiddie pools are for kids. We're looking to dive in, head first, to all the hard-to-talk-about topics, tough questions, and thought-provoking Scriptures. We think this is a good thing, because we're in process. We're becoming. And who we're becoming isn't shallow.

LIFT UP RESPONSIBILITY We are committed to being responsible—doing the right things like recycling and volunteering. And we're also trying to grow in our understanding of what it means to share the gospel, serve the poor, love our neighbors, tithe, and make wise choices about our time, money, and relationships.

ENCOURAGE CONNECTION We're looking for connection with our church, our community, with somebody who's willing to walk along side us and give us a little advice here and there. We'd like opportunities to pour our lives out for others because we're willing to do that walk-along-side thing for someone else, too. We have a lot to learn from people older and younger than us. From the body of Christ.

We're glad you picked up this study. Please come by and visit us at *threadsmedia.com*.

CREATION UNRAVELED
THE GOSPEL ACCORDING TO GENESIS
BY MATT CARTER & HALIM SUH

More than a collection of stories, the Bible tells one story—God's story of bringing us back to Himself after sin infiltrated a good world and caused the unraveling of creation. Join authors Matt Carter and Halim Suh as they examine Genesis 1–11 and explore how the first chapters of the Bible lay the foundation for the gospel of Jesus Christ—the good news of salvation and redemption that we find only in relationship with Him.

Matt Carter serves as lead pastor of The Austin Stone Community Church in Austin, Texas. He is also a cancer survivor, author, and speaker for camps and conferences nationwide. Halim Suh is an elder and pastor of equipping at The Austin Stone Community Church.

MENTOR
HOW ALONG-THE-WAY DISCIPLESHIP WILL CHANGE YOUR LIFE
BY CHUCK LAWLESS

Drawing from biblical examples like Jesus and His disciples and Paul and Timothy, author Chuck Lawless explores the life-transforming process of a mentoring relationship. This study is both a practical and spiritual guide to biblical mentoring, providing easy-to-model life application for how to have and be a mentor.

Chuck Lawless is vice president for Global Theological Advance of the International Mission Board. The author of several books, Dr. Lawless is also president of the Lawless Group, a church consulting firm (thelawlessgroup.com).

THIS CHANGES EVERYTHING
LESSONS FROM JAMES
BY BEN STUART

What does following Christ really look like? How does being a Christian change my life? The answer to these questions is revealed in the Epistle of James. Unfortunately many Christians don't allow their faith in Christ to impact the way they live from day to day. Author and pastor Ben Stuart guides readers through what it means to find our identities in Jesus. By examining the life of James, the half-brother of Jesus, this study offers encouragement and practical ideas for encountering the risen Christ and how He can change everything as we follow Him.

Ben Stuart is the executive director for Breakaway Ministries, a non-denominational, weekly Bible study on the campus of Texas A&M University. He grew up in Houston, Texas, and graduated from Texas A&M University in 1998. Ben has a degree in Historical Theology from Dallas Theological Seminary.

GROUP CONTACT INFORMATION

Name _____ Number _____
Email _____

Name _____ Number _____
Email _____

Name _____ Number _____
Email _____

Name _____ Number _____
Email _____

Name _____ Number _____
Email _____

Name _____ Number _____
Email _____

Name _____ Number _____
Email _____

Name _____ Number _____
Email _____

Name _____ Number _____
Email _____